Oh yes we can!

THE MAN WHO
WOULD NOT BE DEFEATED

Mitchell

THE
MAN
WHO
WOULD
NOT BE
DEFEATED

W Mitchell
with Brad Lemley

WRS
PUBLISHING

A Division of WRS Group, Inc.
Waco, Texas

For information about obtaining a videotape or audio tape of
W Mitchell's speech, "It's Not What Happens to You, It's
What You Do about It," please call: **800/421-4840**

For information about inviting W Mitchell to come to
speak to your organization, please contact:

WRS Speakers Bureau,
P. O. Box 21207, Waco, Texas 76702-1207
Phone 800/299-3366, Fax 817/757-1454

Text © 1993 by W Mitchell and Brad Lemley

All rights reserved. No part of this book may be reproduced or transmitted
in any form or by any means, electronic or mechanical, including
photocopying or recording or by any information storage or retrieval
system, without permission in writing from the publisher.

First published in the United States of America in 1993 by WRS Publishing,
A Division of WRS Group, Inc., 701 N. New Road, Waco, Texas 76710
Book design by Kenneth Turbeville
Jacket design by Talmage Minter

10 9 8 7 6 5 4 3 2

Library of Congress Cataloging-in-Publication Data

Mitchell, W., 1943–
    The man who would not be defeated / W. Mitchell with Brad Lemley.
       p.   cm.
    ISBN 1–56796–026–X : $17.95
    1. Mitchell, W., 1943–   . 2. Mayors—Colorado—Biography.
3. Marines—United States—Biography. 4. Success. I. Title.
CT275.M5664A3 1993
978.8'033'092—dc20
    [B]   93-30632
                                                                          CIP

Dedication

For my mother, Ethel, and my father, Bill:
When people ask me where my strength comes from,
how could I not immediately think of all you've given me?

Uncle Luke, Karen, and Gretchen:
Your love, and the model you showed me of how to
do it best, have made such a difference.

Beaty and Bill:
What a wonderful extra set of parents!

Annie, Rita, and Carol:
When I think of you, I see myself at my best.

Ma:
Gracias y Dios te bendiga.

Blackie:
The helmet was very much appreciated.

June and Nualan:
You picked me up when I fell down.
I will always remember you.

Acknowledgment

In writing your article for *Parade* magazine, Brad Lemley, you've become more than just another interviewer. You have become a friend. And you have your own remarkable story of courage.

I go back and forth between feeling guilty about all the work that you've done in the book and feeling appreciation, because you seemed to capture me (both the good and the bad) so wonderfully. As I read along, I hear my voice and my story, which is one more tribute to the magnificence of your ability to sublimate your own feelings and articulate mine.

I could use up more pages than there are in this book thanking everyone. I would, however, like to mention a few people. Tony Robbins has helped me understand even better how much a person can do if they are willing to access all the areas of the brain that we normally let sleep.

Jim Pancero opened a wonderful door for me. He has not only allowed my voice to be heard by so many more, but has also been a wonderful coach.

Capt. Jerry Coffee is a wonderful friend, and he, too, has given me and a lot of others a wonderful hand up. Many thanks to him.

And the list goes on and on. Suffice it to say, if you've been there for me, I will never forget you, and together we are making an incredible difference.

Foreword

Nothing splendid has ever been achieved
except by those who believed that something inside of
them was superior to circumstances.
—Bruce Barton

If you are familiar with me and with my life's work, then you know that it is my aim to enable you to experience life at its fullest, to realize your own unique form of greatness.

We all have a sleeping giant within us. Each of us has a talent, a gift, a bit of genius just waiting to be tapped. I have recognized the power that we have to change virtually anything and everything in our lives. The amazing thing is that the resources that we need to turn our dreams into reality lie *within us.*

It doesn't matter what advantages or disadvantages you were born with. It's not the *conditions* or the "externals" of your iife that will determine your destiny. What matters is what *decisions* you make about how your life is going to be—the *decisions* that will write the story of your destiny. By making decisions about what to do with your life, you will have become a living example of the unlimited power of the human spirit. You and I can make our lives one of those inspiring examples. How? Simply by making decisions today about how we're going to live in the years to come.

W Mitchell has refused to be overcome by two life-threatening and life-changing accidents—disastrous events, which, if given the power, could have ruled his life to its end. Instead, he decided to make the tragedies that befell him a starting point. When he says, "It's not what happens to you in life, it's what you do about it," you can be sure that he is a living, breathing example of that message to us.

I believe that your desire to expand your own life has brought you to this book about Mitchell—your belief that your own life has the potential to be so much more. I have been inspired by his story myself, because I believe that Mitchell embodies those traits that are required for us to rise above whatever life hands us, those traits that can enable us to be joyful, fulfilled, and whole human beings, created, and always being created, in the image of God.

—Anthony Robbins

Introduction

I have a great life. You can have a great life, too.

You may doubt this. "If only, Mitchell," you might say. "If only I were not so old. So broke. So undereducated. If only my wife/husband/boss/kids would support me in my quest for happiness. I got a raw deal, Mitchell."

To which I simply say: Look at me.

My face looks like a badly made leather quilt; it has inspired children to chant, "Monster, Monster," as I pass. I have no fingers. I cannot walk.

Furthermore, all of this did not happen at once—I did not have the "luxury" of one great, grand accident to get over. *First* I was burned nearly to a crisp; there is probably not one person in a billion who has endured more physical pain than I have. *Then* four years later, in an entirely separate accident, I was paralyzed from the waist down. The average person might call me the unluckiest man alive.

But what I hope to do in this book is teach you *not* to think like the average person. This book—part autobiography, part self-help lesson—aims to show you that *nothing, absolutely nothing* is absolute. Your life is entirely what you decide it is. It is your spaceship, your up, your down. The universe starts in your head and spreads out into the world. Change what happens in your head, and the universe changes.

Really.

I hope to be your touchstone, your route to a new mind. Symbols are potent. The liberty bell conjures the concept of freedom in a single, glowing image. The Taj Mahal shows us, at a glance, the depth and extravagance of human love. The Golden Gate bridge, in my adopted hometown of San Francisco, is a testament to engineering ingenuity that speaks volumes.

I want to be a symbol for you. With my scarred face, my fingerless paws, my wheelchair—and real, genuine happiness in my heart—I want to be your mental image of the power of the human mind to transcend circumstances. As I say in my speeches, "It's not what happens to you, it's what you do about it." When you feel you have met an insurmountable obstacle, I want you to think of me. Then say to yourself, "If he can be successful, I can."

What kind of success are we talking about? I can rattle off my résumé stuff: millionaire, mayor, member of many boards of directors, environmental leader, media personality, political commentator, commercial pilot, in-demand public speaker, even river-rafter and skydiver, but these may not be—probably are not—your measures of success. Nonetheless, whatever you want, you can achieve it, just as I have.

You can because you are not that different from me. I don't have any special powers, any magical gift of birth that has allowed me to create my own happiness in the face of trials. I am no stronger or smarter than the average person. I am a long way from a "saintly" guy. In fact, one of the secrets I'll reveal is that being pushy and generally obnoxious at the right times has been crucial to my success.

Really, the only difference between you and me at the moment is that I had the good fortune to learn a few important points along the way—both before and after my injuries—that helped me immeasurably. In this book, I will pass them along to you. If they have kept me happy, imagine what they will do for you.

I have a great life. You can have a great life, too.

Chapter 1

I believe in heaven and hell—on earth.
—Abraham L. Feinberg

The fireball was about ten feet high and four feet wide. The flame was blue and searing, with the peculiar, intense heat of gasoline burning in the open air. Even standing fifty feet away, on the corner of 26th and South Van Ness, you would have felt the increase in temperature on your face and hands, a warmth that easily cut through San Francisco's gentle, early summer. And you would have had company—a mysterious bonfire in the middle of an urban intersection draws a crowd.

But this is only what I've been told. I can't comment, personally, on the fireball's external dimensions and characteristics.

I was in it.

I'm hazy on the view from inside. One of many nice things about the design of the human brain is that it erases tapes that would be too painful to replay. The actual experience of the fire certainly fits that criterion. But if hell on earth ever existed for real, it was here, on July 19, 1971.

How had it happened?

In retrospect, it was almost like a movie. Just when everything starts going well, the hero gets a pie in the face, a "Dear John" letter, a knife in the back, or a bullet between the eyes. Similarly, the fireball capped the best day of my life.

That morning, I had fulfilled a lifelong dream by soloing in an airplane for the first time; an experience I can only describe as orgasmic.

That afternoon, I was riding my motorcycle. Not just

any motorcycle, this was a Honda 750: at the time the biggest, snazziest, meanest cycle on the market. I had bought it just the day before, and I adored it.

As I rode that morning, I felt grand, and not just because of my new student pilot's license and new wheels. I was twenty-eight years old, handsome (at least I thought so), in perfect health, had a marvelous, romantic job as a cable car gripman, plenty of money, many good friends, a gorgeous girlfriend... it was even a nice day!

In short, I felt like the King of San Francisco, Suzerain of the Realm, and Potentate of the Far Territories as I zoomed up South Van Ness.

South Van Ness is a four-lane street, and I was in the outside lane, heading north. A maroon laundry truck was tooling along next to me in the inside, northbound lane.

As we reached 26th, the laundry truck suddenly turned right, smack in my way, cutting me off. I hit the truck squarely in the side.

I went down, crushing my left elbow and cracking my pelvis. This was serious, but hardly life-threatening.

But the lid on the gas tank popped open, and two-and-a-half gallons of gasoline poured out onto the hot engine, and onto me.

The whole business went up with a WHOOSH. It was a strange sight, a nightmare scene—the kind of scene that freezes people. Though the fireball was visible for blocks, no one acted, at least not at first. They froze. If I had seen it, I might have frozen myself.

But I am here to write this because a man whose name I never learned, a fellow who sold cars at the auto lot at that intersection, grabbed a fire extinguisher and put me out.

The ambulance arrived within three minutes. I imagine that they were three very long minutes. If that memory-tape is still inside me, unplayed, I hope it never does get played. The motorcycle remained too hot to touch even twenty minutes later, when the police were investigating the accident.

At San Francisco General Hospital, which is about ten blocks from the accident scene, I was judged to be at the "low end of survivability." In 1971, if you were burned over seventy-five percent of your body, you were definitely dead. I was burned over sixty-five percent of my body, which put my chances around fifty-fifty. All that had been spared was my scalp, which had been covered by my motorcycle helmet, and most of my torso and arms, which had been protected by my leather jacket.

As the nurses cut my still-smoldering clothes off of me, I went into a coma, one that was quickly deepened by the drugs I was given to lessen my shock. It would be two weeks before I would come around.

So much for the king of San Francisco.

Chapter 2

The joy of the young is to disobey.
—James M. Barrie

Actually, that I should be injured in such a dramatic fashion was not, in retrospect, all that surprising. Since my childhood—when my name was William John Schiff III, but I was usually called "Wild Bill"—I had been possessed of a taste for the dramatic. This was coupled with a hatred for rules. My mother liked to say that I interpreted every "Do Not Enter" sign to read, "Welcome, Billy."

I was born April 11, 1943, into upper-middle-class circumstances in Wallingford, Pennsylvania, the youngest of three children and the only boy.

I have been called unstoppable. If so, I came by it honestly. At age thirteen, my father, William John II, had spent a year in a body cast to mend a frozen hip, during which time his father died and he became the sole support of his mother. Doctors pounded the notion home that he would be unable to do many things that "normal" people could, including play golf. I believe it was their insistence that he would never play the game that made him a devoted player throughout his life.

He was a successful insurance executive and represented upward mobility to my mother, the strikingly beautiful daughter of a stocking factory worker. But he had an explosive temper—another trait I'm afraid I inherited—and they divorced when I was five.

Almost immediately, she married Luke Mitchell, and my life was never the same.

Luke Mitchell was handsome. He looked a good deal like Clark Gable, and cut a dashing figure. He was chivalrous, and a war hero, having served with distinction in the cavalry in World War I. He had once been quite wealthy, but was wiped out financially in the Depression. By the time he came into our lives, he had the kind of balanced perspective that such shifting fortunes can bring.

"Uncle Luke" was strict, sometimes in ways that seem positively antediluvian by today's standards. For example, he found poor grammar in any form intolerable; and in his view, the word "okay" was completely unacceptable. He would mete out extra chores based on grammatical slips; a single "okay" might rate fifteen extra minutes of leaf-raking.

But his punishments were never harsh, and he taught me far more about love than about discipline. I was an "overactive" child, which is to say, I never murdered anyone, but that was more due to clumsiness than lack of intention. From age four, when I filled a neighbor's gas tank with gravel and was frequently found teetering on the peak of our roof, it was clear to everyone that if ever a kid deserved a regular whack on the behind, it was me. But Luke could never bring himself to do it.

Finally, one day I had done something so heinous—I believe I had set the living room curtains afire once too often—that my mother and two older sisters persuaded him that he had to spank me.

So he did. I forgot it in ten minutes and went on to some other dastardly deed, but my mother told me that this war hero, this swashbuckling gentleman, had come to their bedroom crying. It killed him, he said, to have to do that.

But, as I say, I no doubt richly deserved it; and it took many years before his stellar example would bear fruit in my personality. When I was twelve, my parents (I continued to love to be with my father, spending almost every weekend with him, and we remained very close) arranged to have the psychology department of the University of Pennsylvania test me because I was such a terror.

I was bright, no doubt about that. While taking the

train into the city every weekend to see my father, I had insinuated myself into the good graces of the engineers, and actually wound up driving the train. The engineers would let me run the throttle and brakes, and I got quite good at it, which began my lifelong love affair with things fast and mechanical. But, as I say, in the midst of such precocious activity I was flunking out of sixth grade. The psychologists determined that I was a "gifted underachiever." As if to prove their point, I flunked seventh grade, repeated it, and was finally shipped off by my distraught parents to the Augusta Military Academy in Fort Defiance, Virginia, in 1958, when I was fourteen.

I loved it. It was every boy's dream—to march around, carry a gun, be encouraged to be a tough guy. I also liked the fact that academics weren't pushed. The point was to be a stud Marine, a role that fit my adolescent fantasies better than that of bookworm.

Of course, military schools demand discipline, and while I was still rebellious, I was becoming increasingly clever at turning on the smile and not getting caught at misbehaving. "Lights out" at nine meant all power was chopped off in the rooms, but that was only a minor inconvenience to me. I drilled through the wall into the bathroom, ran a wire, hung blankets over my windows and hooked up lights and a radio in my room.

This kind of shenanigan made me a popular guy, but after two years of military academy, my parents figured I had shaped up enough to do tenth grade in a more demanding venue: the Perkioman Preparatory School in Pennsburg, Pennsylvania, about two hours from Philadelphia.

There, I was in hot water almost immediately. For one, I had been smoking since I was twelve; and at Perkioman they were less than thrilled with that habit. Again, academically, I was a disaster. I spent most of that year receiving lectures from the headmaster, and was eventually booted out.

This led to an ignominious return to public school back in Middletown, near my home in Rosetree.

That spring, Luke became aware that he had liver cancer. We spent a lot more time together, just driving around and talking. He didn't say anything magic that I recall; no lectures on the meaning of life echo in my brain. But like some of the most impressive people on earth, he simply had a presence, a bearing, that was unmistakable.

He died in the summer of 1960.

His death hit me like a physical blow. Nothing was going right. I was sure I had flunked tenth grade, and was in no mood to repeat it. I just wanted to get away.

On a hooky-jaunt to Philadelphia with a buddy one day, we went into a Marine Corps recruiting office and got the papers; at seventeen, you need your parents' permission to enlist. My mother was not thrilled, but my father, quite justifiably, thought it was just what I needed, and persuaded her to sign.

Boot camp on Parris Island, South Carolina, found me in my usual quota of hot water: I recall doing seven hundred squat jumps as punishment for some infraction, and having to be helped up the stairs for three days. But I had the advantage of two years of military school behind me; and knowing how to take a rifle apart and similar military basics stood me in good stead. Then, during infantry training in North Carolina, an intelligence test put me in the upper twenty percent of my platoon.

In the Marines, this was no great distinction. For example: because about two-thirds of military life is spent waiting in line, I got into the habit of carrying a book in my pocket to pass the time. I was reading *Hawaii* once, in line at the flamethrower range, and the sergeant had a typical Marine reaction to this display of even moderate intellectual development. Furious, he ordered me to give him the book, and he set it up as my flamethrower target. And I had to torch it. It was a sterling example of the Marine philosophy: if the Corps didn't issue it, you don't need it.

Anyway, this high score—I believe anyone whose knuckles weren't dragging on the ground could have gotten the same—allowed me to go to the Naval Air Station in Jacksonville, Florida, to be trained as an ordinance man—a guy who loads bombs and bullets onto aircraft.

This was better than being an infantry grunt, but it still sounded rather like work. So I managed to stretch an easy, six-month position on the "support staff" of the Jacksonville school to two years before someone noticed I had fallen through the cracks. I was ordered to begin loading ordinance immediately, and I got to choose where. Having never been west of the Mississippi, I picked Hawaii.

In Hawaii's Kaneohe Marine Corps Air Station, I loaded ordinance for the VMA 214, the famous "Black Sheep" squadron that Pappy Boyington assembled in World War II out of brig-dwellers, attitude cases, and sundry military-aviation lowlife, and which went on to serve with distinction. By the time I got there, only the reputation remained, but we all took pride in our rebellious roots. I worked on the A4-D, a single-pilot attack bomber. Despite the military's attempt to cauterize my academic yearnings, I got my General Equivalency Diploma and enrolled in the University of Hawaii, specializing in political science. It was here that I realized that the ideas of Bobby Kennedy and Martin Luther King, Jr., resonated within me more than those of Barry Goldwater.

By 1964, I left the military and completed a transition I had been undergoing from conservative to liberal—by marching in an anti-Vietnam demonstration a month later. I also began work as a bartender, small-business training that was to help me immensely in my later life.

And that December, I got married. My bride was Carol Kaleiwahea, who at twenty-eight was seven years older than me, and whom I had pursued with great vigor. She was gorgeous, and I loved her five-year-old son, Kimo, too.

But the whole affair was emblematic of my impetuous nature. At twenty-one, the idea of being forever bonded to someone I had known only briefly made me panicky. After we had been married about six months, I decided we needed to be divorced.

This was completely my idea, and she was amazed. She reluctantly agreed, and we got the divorce. Although she initially wanted nothing more to do with me, I convinced her to continue together with me as a family. I am not particularly proud of this episode, especially considering that the crux of my message to audiences today is that we must take responsibility for our actions. I think one reason I push the idea so strongly is that I remember the pain I caused as a callow youth by failing to take responsibility.

While still bartending, I also worked as a producer (which meant I fetched iced tea) for disk jockey Marc Smith for KGU Radio. I progressed rapidly, and soon was doing my own jazz show, interviewing greats like Thelonius Monk, who did not seem to notice (or was kind enough to avoid noticing) that I didn't know the first thing about jazz. Working in radio had long been a dream of mine, but at $2.50 an hour, the bills were not getting paid. Though technically divorced, I felt a family obligation to get a real job, so in 1967 we packed up and went back to Philadelphia, where I got a job in my father's insurance firm.

It's hard to say who was more miserable in Philly: Carol, an island free-spirit stuck in suburban Philadelphia, or me, a young buck with a wild streak forced to read and understand the most boring product on the planet. (If you ever have trouble falling asleep, curl up with "The Standard Fire Policy.") After eight months of foot-dragging, I was "offered the opportunity to seek other avenues" five minutes before they fired me.

Carol, desperately missing Hawaii, left with Kimo, and I was footloose again. I had done volunteer work for Robert Kennedy's presidential campaign, and Blackie Burak, a buddy from the Marines, suggested we head to California, ostensibly to help with the upcoming primary election effort there, but perhaps more because, in 1968, San Francisco was the place for a young person to be.

Blackie was a law student, and one day in California we wandered into the Law Library at Hastings. We dug out the books and discovered that California was the only remaining state that allowed a common-law name change. I had already started to use "Mitchell" as a nickname, in memory of Luke. Now, I saw an unconventional way to make it official, so I changed my name to William Mitchell simply by having that name put on my new, California driver's license.

But my real aim was for people to call me just "Mitchell." I wanted to hear that name often, to remind me of him, and work to make myself more like him. I pursued this aim by shortening my new name to "W. Mitchell," but people kept asking what the "W." stood for. So I extracted the period and became, legally, W Mitchell, with the W, officially, not standing for anything.

The day we arrived was probably the last great day of the hippy revolution. Working as a cab driver, I spent a lot of time in the Haight-Ashbury district, and could easily see its slow decline. But my life was about to enter a wonderful new chapter.

I became a cable car gripman.

A San Francisco cable car gripman has a job unlike any other in the world, because cable cars are unlike any other kind of transportation. These cars have no motor; they are propelled by gripping a cable that slides along under the street at ten miles per hour. The "grip" is the gadget that hangs down from the center of the cable car and the gripman pulls and pushes this to make it grab and release the cable.

In the modern world, it is one of the most swashbuckling jobs you can get—perfect for a swashbuckling type like me. You wear an anachronistic uniform, sort of a cross between an American cop and a French Foreign Legionnaire. You pilot the most unusual and well-known examples of public transportation on the globe. You are surrounded by people who are generally in a good mood. It's tough to be depressed on a cable car. Because folks have generally never seen a cable car gripman before, they come to you without expectations. However you behave, there's a good chance they'll forgive you.

I played it to the hilt. I worked out a deal with a street-side flower vendor: Each day, I would buy a gross of his day-old roses for ten bucks. I stashed them in the car and distributed them during the day to all the women riders, until I ran out. I also carried a little camera, and took photos of the wonderful, bright smiles of the loveliest women, from ages two to eighty, who rode in my car. These cheap, shameless ploys for female attention never failed. I was always swimming in girlfriends.

The job had its hazardous side as well, which to me was part of its appeal. On one occasion, my grip welded itself to the cable—this happens sometimes, due to the intense friction and heat—and as I frantically tried to release it, my car crunched a Karmann Ghia like an accordion! (The driver was hysterical but unhurt.)

The gripman always has to be on the lookout for a "jump"—when the grip on a stationary car does not grab the cable gradually, but seizes it, actually lifting the whole, seven-ton car off the ground and instantly hurling it forward at ten miles an hour. Evel Knievel, the motorcycle stuntman, used to say that his motorcycle was the fastest thing on Earth except for a cable car catching a jump.

The most dramatic example of a jump occurred in the 1940s, when a driver was backing down a hill, caught the cable, and rocketed up the hill so quickly that sailors on the car were left standing in the street, still holding the stanchions.

I'm happy to report this never happened to me.

I fell into a wonderful routine. I would work the cable cars for sixteen hours at a stretch, seven days a week, loving every minute of it. When I had saved enough—which was easy, as the job paid the princely sum of $5 per hour—I would light out for Colorado to ski with my girlfriend Rita Salcedo, who at that point was, technically, my common-law wife.

It was a fun, though rather self-centered existence; I certainly wasn't giving Albert Schweitzer anything to worry about. And thus I might have spent my life. But, as the author Larry McMurtry says, life is a twisting river; and for me, many twists lay ahead.

Chapter 3

W

*Personally, I'm always ready to learn,
though I do not always like being taught.*
—Winston Churchill

As I said, I was no humanitarian along the lines of Albert Schweitzer; I was no philosopher in the mold of Schopenhauer either. My philosophical underpinning was, essentially, "The Universe is incomprehensible. Have fun, and try to be a nice guy."

But this began to erode and be replaced by something rather more comprehensive and useful: a philosophy/theology/concept called "Morehouse."

This was one of the first "head trips" that were popping up in California in those early days of the counterculture; EST and Lifespring are two better-known ones that came along later. It's common in these jaded days to pooh-pooh these things, but the fact is that they contained valuable information.

Carl Burak, Blackie's cousin, encouraged us to attend a session in a private home on Sacramento Street. Most of these movements have a leader, and this one was no different. A charismatic guy named Victor Baranco was running the show.

Over the next few weeks, I went to many sessions. I skipped the cult aspects—Victor struck me as an interesting guy, but I felt no particular attraction—but the information was fascinating and useful.

Morehouse's thrust was three-fold:

First, you are perfect. In other words, even when you are doing asshole—and I do asshole excellently—you are perfect at that moment. You are fine. You are a human being, being yourself. Many of us fruitlessly aspire to be a cool, flawless, constantly happy, totally in-control person, but that is an idiotic aspiration that creates a lot of misery. Real people get sad, angry, feel grief, say things they regret.

I resisted this. So a child abuser is perfect when he's beating a kid? So Hitler was perfect when he was gassing the Jews? It seemed like pure nonsense, even dangerous nonsense.

But Morehouse was introducing the idea in an extreme way to help people accept the kernel of truth behind it: that by accepting yourself, you allow yourself to move on; you are not forever trapped in a web of self-hatred. The thinking of someone who has mastered this concept is: "Yesterday, I blew up at you, I was doing asshole perfectly. Today, I will give you these flowers, I will show you another side of me." If you cannot accept your negative aspects—if you dwell on them, wallowing in regret—you are actually reinforcing them, and you might never succeed in getting beyond them. Eventually, asshole may become a smaller and smaller part of who you are. For my part, people who have known me for a long time tell me I am not nearly so skilled at asshole as I once was. I believe I am losing my expertise mostly because I no longer dwell on it. I have stopped the training program.

Second, there is no absolute relationship between any two variables. In other words, rich, famous, and surrounded by friends does not automatically equal happy; poor, unknown, and alone does not automatically equal miserable. These may be the social, cultural definitions, but they breed untold despair, as few people can achieve all the "requirements" for happiness. Morehouse's point was that you are driving your own spaceship, and—within legal boundaries, one would hope—you can choose an entirely different set of requirements. You are free to decide that wealth and fame are stultifying, whereas poverty and anonymity are liberating: the late John Belushi is an example of the legitimacy of the former idea; Mother Theresa shows us the truth embodied in the latter. You are free to look at every difficulty that life brings your way as a challenge rather than a setback. You are free to do what feels right to you, rather than what you have been told to do. The point is to take charge of your situation.

Third, you are responsible for your life. There is never any point in looking for the bad guy, the rotten "other" upon whom you can heap blame for your wretched situation. No matter how guiltless you may seem to be, no matter how carefully you document the unjust abuses heaped upon you, you and only you are the only one who can turn your life around. So you'll do better if you adopt the belief or at least explore the possibility that, at some level, you brought it on yourself. Seeking the villain who screwed you is a pointless pursuit; it robs you of the energy you could be using to improve your life.

Again, this sounded a bit flaky at first. Some nut stabs you in the back as you stroll down a street in broad daylight, and it's your own fault? A meteor lands on your head and you are to blame? But the kernel of truth was here, too: that you, and only you, are having the experience. If you wish to extricate yourself from the experience and get on with your life, you must use your energy in a productive way, and you can only do that if you take responsibility. Hunting down folks to blame is not productive. Taking whatever lessons this experience taught you and going on from there is productive. It is the only course that makes sense.

I did not instantly become an enlightened master as a result of my involvement with Morehouse. On the surface, I am sure I remained the selfish galoot I had always been. But I could see the deep truth in these ideas, and they percolated slowly into my subconscious.

Chapter 4

I'm not afraid to die.
I just don't want to be there when it happens.
—Woody Allen

None of this was in the forefront of my mind in San Francisco General Hospital. Nothing was in the forefront, or on the back burner, for that matter. I had—fortunately—lapsed into a coma, one that was quickly deepened by a variety of tranquilizing drugs that prevented me from feeling my pain and going into deeper shock.

As I say, I was burned over sixty-five percent of my body. Virtually every part of me except for my scalp, which was protected by my motorcycle helmet, and my torso, which was shielded by my leather jacket, was red-and-black charred meat.

I am fuzzy on the first two weeks. The doctors were fuzzy too—on whether I would survive. I was in a private room, and was tended round the clock.

I looked horrific. An appropriate question, I'm told, for a stranger seeing me for the first time was not Who is it? but, rather What is it? The burns were bad enough; add to that the fact that my eyelids were sewn shut to keep my eyes moist; I had a tracheotomy tube inserted into my throat to help me breathe; and my weight quickly plummeted from 175 to 125; and you have a pretty ghastly specimen. I have heard that visitors, including tough guys with whom I had worked on the cable cars, would faint upon seeing me.

My sister Karen was one of the first family members who arrived from the East Coast, and I don't even remember her being there. Words floated at me from the stream of visitors: "Hang in there," "You're going to make it," and most frequently, "What can I do to help?" Of course, they were already doing just the right thing. Hearing the warm voices of friends through the midst of semiconsciousness was probably the main thing that kept me going at that stage.

Slowly, I started to swim up out of it. But once I became completely conscious, I wondered if consciousness was such a terrific idea.

I could see nothing. I was told I was lying in bed with my hands and arms completely swathed in bandages and elevated in slings. My legs were also raised. They were swollen to twice their normal size, a macabre patchwork of black-and-red flesh.

Writers can exhaust themselves searching for metaphors for pain, but I think the man who eventually did most of my reconstructive plastic surgery, Dr. Mark Gorney, put it best: "Being extensively burned is the most catastrophic, painful, unimaginably difficult situation a human being can find himself in. In terms of pain, it is like being flayed alive every day."

I agree.

To be sure that I did not completely despair, (at this stage, one stays alive through sheer willpower) mirrors were kept away from me after my eyelid-sutures were removed. I knew that my face, which was only partially bandaged, was badly burned, and I surmised that it was pretty gruesome; a succession of visitors who grimace and/or pass out at the sight of your countenance quickly gives you that impression. But I knew, intuitively, that I'd have to ration my challenges. Now, the point was staying alive. I would demand a mirror in good time.

Simply existing with these burns was difficult, and any kind of movement was particularly excruciating. One of my "fondest" memories was the trip to the whirlpool, where I was often taken to help me shed dead skin. San Francisco General is an old building, and its floors have multiple cracks, seams, thresholds, and bumps, everyone of which sent a tremor through my body. There was one particular buckle in the linoleum on that trip that I remember too well. The gurney would hit it, and pain would shoot through every part of my body.

This, in fact, is what makes the pain of being burned so extreme: you will die from fluid loss or infection if you are left alone, so you are never left alone. Something terribly painful is being done to you virtually every hour of the day, day after day. Skin is whirlpooled away, grafted back on, stretched, squeezed, lubricated, bandaged, poked for intravenous feeding... I had sixteen skin-graft surgeries in four months! If you *started* this process one-hundred percent healthy, you'd soon be pushed to the limit. When you start it in agony and three-fourths dead, it is truly no picnic.

This was exemplified when, after about a month, I turned to my nurse, June Fulbright, and said, quietly, "I've died. I am dead. This is all a fantasy. I didn't survive the accident at all. I'm actually dead."

From my perspective, it seemed the only rational conclusion. I had never been out of my room, except for surgeries and whirlpool therapies. I had never been able to look out of a window. I never saw anything, really, but a fuzzy view of the ceiling. While my contact lenses saved my vision when I went up in flames, the corneas were still badly burn-scarred and cloudy at this point.

Fortunately, June recognized this syndrome, which sometimes strikes people who have undergone extremely traumatic injury and pain. While the conscious mind understands, the more primitive parts of the brain conclude that, given such extraordinary pain, the result must soon be death. After a while, these subconscious forces conclude that enough time has passed now; now, I must *be* dead.

I'm no medical expert, but I know that voodoo can kill if the "cursed" person strongly believes a deadly spell has been put on him. Given my strong belief and my still-weak condition, anything might have happened.

So June did the right thing. She immediately loaded me onto a gurney and wheeled me outside. She also called Rita, and had her bring our dog, this 125-pound Great

Dane we called "Puppy," to see me. She spoke quickly, forcefully: "Look, see the trees, see the sky, see the people, see the city? This is reality. This is the real world full of living people, and you are one of them. You are alive; you are very much alive."

It worked. I understood. The fresh air and view of the city were like smelling salts to me. It was like a giant whiff of reality.

Incidentally, I'm told that Puppy went nuts when he heard my voice, but could not see anyone he recognized as his master, either by sight or smell. I was just an odd shape on the gurney, and the sound of my voice made him lunge in every direction searching for me. June was panicked that Puppy was going to jump on the gurney and try to dig down through me to find his master. She didn't let the dog come back to the hospital for some time.

Once it appeared there was a pretty good chance of my surviving, the focus of attention turned to my fingers. They were black, and the tips were dead. I have pictures of me at the time, which were to be used in court, but the judge ruled that they were inadmissible because they were too inflammatory, so to speak. Much of the tissue was dead, and needed to be removed. I recall one of the only two times I asked for morphine was when an intern attempted to remove some of that skin. To this day, that was one of the most painful episodes I can recall.

They were, indeed, pretty grotesque, black and twisted, and the surgeons determined that it was essential to remove that dead skin, so they scheduled me for surgery. When I came back from the surgery on them, I was feeling pretty confident. I knew that the surgeon had removed the parts of the fingers that were no longer viable, but I could feel, within the thick gauze bandages, that the fingers were still there. I could feel my fingertips; I could even move them.

"Wow," I told June Fulbright, my nurse, "they really didn't have to remove much at all."

She said "Uh-huh," and excused herself.

June and Nualan Shaw were "private duty" nurses, brought in for special situations in which the patient needs round-the-clock care.

Nurses who accept burn cases are a special breed, because it is so extraordinarily painful to care for the patient, and the patients often die. Even among these exceptional people, June and Nualan were among the best. During the four months that they took care of me, Nualan took six days off, June took three days.

They were absolutely devoted to me, and I to them. I give them a great deal of credit for my survival. The preached wisdom is that patients do better if the staff is not personally involved. My wisdom, and that of my nurses, was that patients do better only if the staff *is* personally involved. Bleaching friendship out of a hospital, where doctors, nurses, and patients tend to be people, is foolish, and usually, thank goodness, impossible.

I learned later that both June and Nualan had seen the operation, and both had cried at the sight. So after three days of listening to me blather about how wonderful it was to still have my fingers, they went to the doctors and said, "Look, you idiots, talk to Mitchell."

But none of the doctors had the guts to tell me the truth. Finally, one day, a resident came in and said it was time to unwrap the bandages. As he did this, he pointed out that "We had to remove more tissue than we thought we would," and "Phantom limbs can make you feel as if something is still there when it is actually gone."

There was a fair amount of tension in the room. I vividly remember him unwrapping my hands. He seemed to unwrap for longer than was possible. Even after the bandages were fist-sized, he kept unraveling for a long time.

Finally, he was done. I had no fingers. All that remained were little stumps, the largest perhaps a half-inch long. The room was silent for awhile.

"Wow," I said at last. "This is going to destroy my pool game."

Well, what could I say? "I'm gonna strangle you, you

jerk"? The guy had done the best he could. Anyway, it's tough to strangle someone when you don't have fingers.

The normal, expected, even encouraged reaction would be to moan, wail, cry, curse God, sink into a funk, maybe even commit suicide.

But like the bumper sticker says, "Why be normal?"

I thought of the support of my family and friends. I thought of my Marine Corps training. I thought about Morehouse, and how there was no absolute relationship between any two variables. Once I had fingers. Now I didn't. Whatever meaning this change had would be the meaning I gave it. I could see it as a catastrophe, or as a challenge.

I chose the latter.

Chapter 5

The first and great commandment is,
don't let them scare you.
—Elmer Davis

My mother was in Europe at the time of the accident, and, perhaps lacking a complete picture of the extent of the burns or heeding the advice of my sister, did not come to see me until after I had been in the hospital a month. After visiting me, she sent a note to Rita, commenting upon how positive and optimistic I seemed. "But what's he going to do when he realizes how terrible it is?" she concluded.

She did not know, but I knew, even then: the secret to survival was consciously *not* realizing how terrible it was. More than two decades later, I am proud to say that I still refuse to "know" how terrible it was; in other words, to adopt the social definition of what being so horribly burned "should" mean. If you have a difficult situation in your life, I suggest you refuse to realize how terrible it is, too. How about realizing what can be salvaged? How about realizing what you have learned? How about realizing that the worst is behind you? How about...

After a month of weakness and passivity, I decided to take control of my situation. I cannot overemphasize how important it is to do this. Numerous studies have shown that people will forego food, sleep, sex, and almost any other hunger you can imagine before they will give up control. Control and well-being are so intimately related they are almost synonymous.

I took control in two major ways.

First, a move was afoot to transfer me out of San Francisco General and into a state-of-the-art burn unit at

St. Francis General Hospital operated by Dr. Marc Gorney, a highly respected plastic surgeon. When Marc came into my room, I immediately noticed how the other doctors deferred to him. It was clear that he was the top dog in the world of burn rehabilitation.

He looked me over, and it was obvious that he thought I was getting second-rate care; as he put it later, "Mitchell was dying by inches." He said, briskly, "We need to transfer you to our burn unit. We'll send the ambulance this afternoon."

It seemed a wonderful windfall. I was excited about the chance to get the best care available. Then, I casually mentioned that it would be exciting having June and Nualan there too, as they would enjoy working in such modern conditions.

He, just as casually, said that would not be necessary. He wouldn't need them. He had his own team.

I responded, rather less casually, "I have my team too. We have spent a lot of time together. I trust and respect these people. I want them to come."

Again, he briskly told me he knew what was best and that I would not miss them at all.

There was a pause. Then, I thanked him for coming. I told him I would not be going to St. Francis Hospital. I was satisfied at San Francisco General.

This was a guy who was used to getting his own way. He was amused. He figured I was delirious from the burns and medication, and he strolled away, determined to save my life despite my idiocy.

Later, I learned that there was a conference between my attorneys, my family, and Mark Gorney. One of my legal staff, John Brennan, said they could go into court and get an order to declare me incompetent and move me whether I wanted to be moved or not. I think the best thing that happened to me during my whole stay at San Francisco General was that that plan fell through. The loss of control and the loss of two people who had become so important to me could have been fatal. I am a survivor, but at that moment, I did not need another test.

Second, I began managing my own care. After two months of the excruciating physical pain of endless pokes and prods, wrappings and unwrappings, I asked for the chief of staff.

"I need some time off," I told him. "I can't do this anymore. I am exhausted. I have to stop."

He said he understood. With me, he went through the treatment schedule step by step, looking for any way to cut back on the almost continuous treatments. He promised they would do whatever they could do to cut back. He also promised that, from then on, he would explain the reasons for everything that was done to me.

It helped immeasurably. Dressing changes were shifted from every three hours to every four; whirlpool treatments from daily to every other day. The reduction in pain was, probably, fairly minor, but the real plus was that I was gaining some control.

The turning point for me was the afternoon the plastic surgeon came in to see me.

"Mitchell," he said, "it's time we talked about your face. Your original face has been burned off. We need to make you a new one. What did you look like before? Do you have some pictures?"

June remembered that my wallet had survived the fire. She took it from a drawer and gave it to the surgeon. He rummaged around in it until he found my driver's license.

He stared at the photo on the license for a long time. Then he stared at me. Then he looked back at the license.

"Man," he said finally. "I know we can do better than this."

I laughed. It hurt like hell, but I laughed. For the first time in two months, I found some humor in my life. At that moment, I began to gain some perspective. It may be that, at that moment, the seeds were planted of the message that I share with so many people around the world today: it's not what happens to you, it's what you do about it.

After two months, I could walk, but only barely. Walking to the door, which was about twelve feet from the bed, remains, to this day, the hardest thing I have ever done. I asked Nualan to put a piece of gauze around my hand, then put a pen in the gauze, then put some hospital tape on the door. I made a mark on the door. When the chief of staff came in the next day, I proudly pointed to my mark in the tape. He smiled. I cried. I was going to get better.

Then, after three months, skin was grafted to the backs of my legs. It was one of the last grafting operations, and from then on, I was a racehorse. I was walking all over the place!

Before long, I started walking to the bathroom in the ward. Because I still needed help to handle things, nurses would always go with me, and they would carefully steer me away from the mirrors.

I still had not seen my face. I figured I was ready. I said to June, "I just saw Joe out in the hall. Could you ask him to come over for a second?" She was halfway out before she realized that Joe was not there and that this was just a ruse so I could get to the mirror.

I looked.

Today, I look like a movie star compared to the guy who looked back at me from that mirror. The scars were so graphic. It looked as though my face had been sewn together by a clumsy seamstress working in a hurry in a dark room. The nose was partially collapsed, my eyes looked out of ragged, misshapen holes.

"Woooo," I said softly. "That's an interesting-looking guy."

Naturally, I was shocked. But, somehow, I wasn't horrified by it. I had my bedrock of information—that *I* would decide what to do about this, not society—and that held me together. Under it all, I had the strong sense that I would get through this.

After four months, I was ready to go. Looking back on my survival, I realized that the Morehouse principals had served me well.

But I also learned something that Morehouse had not mentioned. America is very much a paddle-your-own-canoe nation, and Morehouse, with its emphasis on the ability of a single person to create his or her own reality, fit into that quite well.

But there are times when we cannot do it alone. Without those doctors, nurses, relatives, and friends giving me their skill and their love, I am sure that even the most elegant, self-contained philosophical system could not have saved me. In particular, I was aided all along by my Rita's mother, Beatrize Bernal, who came every single day to visit me, and who came to regard me as a son. I also remember a hospital janitor named Joe Williams. Even when he wasn't working on my floor, he would come up, stick his head in my room, and say, "Mitchell! You're looking a little better, Man! Don't quit! Come on, Mitchell!"

So, to ideas I've already mentioned about coping and growing through adversity, let me add a crucial factor:

Support. We all need people who care. Almost anything can be borne if one feels surrounded by a network of friends and family, whereas a minor setback can derail a person who is trying to muscle through life alone. And friendships don't just happen, they must be actively started and actively maintained, or they wither.

It took my utter helplessness to let me see this clearly, but we all have areas in which we are helpless. Whatever you are going through: do what you can on your own, but don't be afraid to reach out for help. Putting both inner and outer resources together is an unbeatable combination.

Chapter 6

*In such a strait the wisest may well be perplexed
and the boldest staggered.*
—Edmund Burke

After my four months in the hospital, obviously, I was a new being. I had gone from a guy who owned the city to one who could not zip his fly. It was clear that I needed help. Bea Bernal offered it, putting me up in the best room of her modestly appointed home in San Francisco's Mission District.

Bea is a living example of the range, power, and depth that love can reach. As a single mother putting a daughter through college, she worked double shifts at a bottle factory in Oakland. Yet during my hospitalization, she managed to visit every single day.

Every day, that is, until one period about three months into my stay in the hospital. When her absence stretched to three days, I got frantic and had the nurses call her home. The word that came back was that she had fallen from the kitchen table and hurt herself. Lying in the hospital, I just couldn't imagine what had happened. All I could guess was that it must have been one wild party.

When, a week later, I actually went into Bea's home because the doctors wanted me to sample the outside world and people's reactions to me, I saw what had really happened. She had painted the entire inside of her home, because doctors had told her that I was at risk for infection and that absolute cleanliness was needed. She had passed out from exhaustion, standing on the table, painting the ceiling while preparing her home for me.

Of all the people I have known, Beatrize, or "Ma" as I call her today, is the one who comes closest to embodying that most challenging of human emotions: unconditional love.

The "couldn'ts" go on and on. With no fingers, and what remained of my hands so sensitive that even a stiff breeze against them was agony, I could not feed myself, drive, turn on a TV, answer a telephone, open a door, reach into my pocket. It was to be six months before I could relieve myself without help.

I grew furious with my inability to do things. I remember lying on my back, screaming and crying, staring at a doorknob I absolutely could not turn. I have never felt more useless.

Then, as I lay there, an idea came to me. I kicked off my slippers, reached up with my feet, and turned the knob.

It was another turning point. As that knob turned and the door swung gently open, the message was slowly starting to crystallize. I had let myself out of another prison. It's not what happens to you, it's what you do about it.

Each day, I learned to do more. Soon, I could eat, using a strap to hold the fork to my hand. I could operate the TV with my toes. Rita graciously filled in the gaps; she dressed me, fed me, got things pointed in the right direction when mounting hydraulic pressure overcame my embarrassment in the bathroom.

But my club-shaped hands and the physical barriers within Beatrize' house, were not the biggest obstacles to overcome. The biggest was my face.

Since that time, I have had literally dozens of operations that include taking hair-bearing skin from the back of my head to create eyebrows, and an agonizingly slow "walk" of skin from under my right arm to my upper chest to alleviate a tight, pulled-down look to my face that made me look particularly macabre. Time has also softened the glaring red color of the new skin grafts and mellowed the raw scars. In short, today, I look like Robert Redford compared to what I looked like then.

I had not spent much time out in the general public, and when I had, I was acutely self-conscious. This society puts a huge premium on facial appearance. Daily, we're awash in TV images of facial perfection: from Christie Brinkley's cheekbones to Kevin Costner's jawline, all adorned with makeup and carefully lit. The subconscious, that great, potent, dumb beast that dwells beneath our everyday minds and runs our lives, absorbs all of these images. It comes to believe, childishly, that these are "normal," and if the image in the mirror does not resemble those on the screen, that we don't measure up.

I was as brainwashed by this fare as anyone. I had been somewhat vain about my looks and had even had a chin implant about a year before the accident to shore up what I thought was a less-than-perfect profile. So my reticence was understandable. When people begin to believe, albeit subconsciously and foolishly, that Tom Selleck is a "normal-looking" fellow, who can blame a guy who looks like he's been whacked with a red-hot meat tenderizer for being a little shy?

So, when I did go outside, I would not meet people's eyes, feeling that perhaps I was doing them a favor; if I didn't look at them, they would be spared the trauma of looking at me.

But I refused to be my face's prisoner. It would have been easy to justify sitting and watching the tube day after day—after all, getting flambéed is a hell of a strain on the system, and sometimes just being alive felt tiring. But I knew, subconsciously anyway, that it was crucial to get out. This was going to be my face for the rest of my life. I had gotten somewhat used to it. Now it was the world's turn.

First came my girlfriend, Rita.

She had been wonderful throughout this ordeal. Our relationship had been strained before the accident, and for that I take much of the blame. As one example: on the night of the accident, when my leather jacket was cut off of my body, a book spilled out. It was a book I had planned to give to a new lady I had met, and the odds had been high that we were going to spend the night together. This was pretty typical behavior for me. I liked the ladies, and never managed anything resembling monogamy through the four years Rita and I were together.

Worse, I had a hell of a temper. Rita still remembers the time my dog Kalani was whining to go outside at three in the morning and I flew into a rage, screaming that I would pitch the dog from the balcony of our third-floor apartment. Yet, to Rita, who was nineteen when we met, I also represented a worldliness and sophistication she had never seen, and I did have a tender side as well. She did love me.

So, though I believe our relationship would have officially and permanently ended the very week of the accident, Rita stayed with me for two more years, and was my primary caretaker.

This was not a fun job. My temper, always a problem, became worse in the early weeks after my release: if the pen and paper were not beside the telephone in their customary positions, I flew into a screaming rage.

Yet she stayed. Looking back, she says she did so out of a combination of compassion and a hope—vain, as it turned out—that her devotion would finally show me how much she loved me and what an idiot I'd be to let her go.

By the time the awful sensitivity of the fresh burns had passed, our sex life eventually returned to normal, but it was difficult. I felt completely impotent, in general, around women. I felt, at the worst, repulsive, and at the best, emasculated. But, because of Rita, that fear slowly passed. The fact that I looked like the most hideous ghoul Stephen King could dream up—not to mention the fact that my income-producing ability had shrunk to nil, perhaps for the rest of my life—mattered not at all to her.

Rita continued the lesson in love that Luke Mitchell had started.

Chapter 7

*The chief cause of human errors is to be found in the
prejudices picked up in childhood.*
—René Descartes

Out in the real world, I walked quite a bit to build my
strength back up. It must have been quite a show.

I had "Puppy," my huge, male Great Dane that I had
trained to heel without a leash before I was burned. He
walked with me everywhere. And because the plastic
surgeons kept emphasizing that I should not get too much
sun, I would wear a hat I had acquired in Aspen: it was a
drill instructor's hat, a "Smokey the Bear" hat.

Well, the sight must have been unbelievable. This
monster dog, and this emaciated, burned up, fingerless
guy with long hair and a drill instructor's hat, strolling
the boulevards of San Francisco. In a city full of weird-
looking folks, especially in those Haight-Ashbury days, I
must have ranked among the weirdest.

The sight obviously did overload a few circuits. I
remember three cases in particular.

Once, I walked to the hospital to visit some patients.
The nurses had actually put me to work, making the
rounds of burn patients. I told them things like "Man,
you're the only guy in this place who's as funny-looking
as I am," as a way to help them gain some perspective.
Perhaps this was the start of my sharing the message: It's
not what happens to you, it's what you do about it.

Anyway, on this particular trip, I told Puppy to stay at
the entrance. He was very good about this. He simply
would not move, and at 125 muscular pounds, few people
were inclined to move him.

When I came out, Puppy was gone. But a man

staggered up, obviously drunk, and started to berate me.

"God, you're a mess. Jesus, you're the ugliest thing I ever saw. What the hell do you think you're doing here? I'm gonna beat that ugly face of yours," he railed at me.

Despite the guy's condition, and the fact that he was probably twenty years older than me, there was simply no way I could have defended myself. I had been a superb physical specimen, an excellent skier, a cable-car gripman, a guy who never had anything to fear. To feel so defenseless was a new and not particularly pleasant sensation. When I said nothing, he got more abusive as he realized I was not going to fight back.

Just as he was ready to begin, I noticed my dog had reappeared. So I said, "Look, I'm pretty messed up. I won't be a match for you. But would you like to fight with my buddy?"

He said, "Sure."

I said "Puppy, come, I want you to meet this guy, because he wants to fight with you." The fellow took one look at this dog, froze for an instant, and then took off so fast I'm not sure even Puppy could have caught him.

It was an early, but classic example of what was to become my overriding philosophy: Do whatever it takes. In this case, the simple solution—pounding the guy into hamburger—was denied to me, so I had to get creative. What would I have done if Puppy had not bounded up?

Perhaps I would have started a conversation with the guy. Maybe I would have enlisted the aid of a bystander. I could have zipped back inside the hospital. At every moment, we have more options than we can imagine; and one good thing that comes from handicaps is that it opens one's eyes to the reality of that.

In any case, this guy was an example of the kind of garbage that gets poured into some unfortunate people's brains, usually when they are children and can't ward it off. Such profoundly insensitive people are, fortunately, rare.

But even "sensitive" people can cause problems.

Because my hands were so incredibly tender in those days, I stood with them in front of me—as if I were carrying a big package with both arms—so that they would not brush my legs. Once, as I stood on a street corner like that, waiting for the light to change, an old, Hispanic man, dressed as if he had very little money to spare, took out some change and put it in my hand.

This was a difficult situation for many reasons, not the least of which was that holding those coins hurt like hell! Beyond that, I did not want to offend the guy. I realized the picture I must be presenting to people. If it happened now, I would simply give the man his money back as politely as I possibly could, explaining that I appreciated the offer, but I did not need it. But then, I simply did not know what to do, and by the time I figured it out, he was gone. (I might add that it's not pure coincidence that the man was poor and Hispanic. I have found since that it is the blacks, the Hispanics, and the down-and-out who generally make eye contact with me on the street; perhaps out of some intuitive sense of sharing a position on the fringes of society. In the worst ghetto in America, I am not only without fear, but I feel welcomed.)

But the most distressing situation arose as Puppy and I walked passed a grade-school playground. One kid spotted me, shouted something to the others, and soon they all broke off their playing and ran to the fence to stare at me. Then, by twos and threes at first, but soon en masse, they chanted: "Monster, monster, monster, monster..."

Teachers swooped down on them immediately, herding them inside, admonishing them that such behavior was impolite.

But I was struck by a feeling of loss. I was not offended by what they had said. I did, indeed, resemble a monster a child might have seen in a movie: rather like Freddy Kruger with a few Frankenstein stitches thrown in.

But I had an overwhelming desire to show them a vital truth: that someone who looks monstrous on the outside can be good, warm, funny, and caring on the inside, someone you might like as well as you like your best friend. I knew that chewing out those kids for their boorishness would not be half as effective as gently and personally *showing* them their honest mistake, that there was a good person under all that scar tissue. I wanted to tell them something that a wonderful speaker and good friend shared with me much later, that the wrapping might have been damaged, but the gift inside was still in good shape.

I think at that moment I subconsciously resolved to make sharing that message with people, especially kids, the focus of my life.

Chapter 8

Even if you're on the right track,
you'll get run over if you just sit there.
—Will Rogers

At the time, however, I was strongly focused on getting my life back into gear. The traditional way one does this is by slowly, cautiously, doing simple tasks until they become easy, then progressing to the harder stuff, all the while remembering that there are now many things the newly handicapped person can *never* do.

That's traditional. It's also idiotic.

Almost immediately, I started ground school, aiming to fly again. I couldn't feed myself, but I refused to focus on just surviving. I planned to thrive, and for me, that meant flying.

Within six months of the burns, at the stage where I still had a hell of a time buttoning my pants, I was flying again with an instructor in Hayward, California, across the bay from San Francisco.

It was awkward. Fingers are definitely handy for pilots. In the cockpit of even a small airplane, there are at least thirty knobs and dials to adjust. There are also fuel controls, rudder and flap switches, and many other small items demanding digital dexterity. Grabbing the microphone now required two hands, which meant letting go of the control column (steering wheel) of the plane every time I needed to chat with the tower, an act which tends to make passengers go pale. My instructor at Hayward Airport could see this, and this is when I saw most clearly that people will do everything for you if you let them.

This is always a tough problem. Most people are naturally helpful, and many with disabilities go along with that helpfulness. The problem, of course, is that it is easy to depend on it, and thus to become increasingly helpless.

Again, the only solution is simply to take charge. Each time I flew, I took care to do one more thing that the instructor had handled on the previous flight. Eventually, I got him to sit back and go along for the ride.

Finally, when we had been flying together for perhaps fifty hours, I was doing well, as well as I had before the accident.

"When are you going to let me solo?" I asked.

"I don't know if you will be allowed to solo," he said. "I'll have to check with the FAA."

So he gets on the phone to the FAA and he says, "This guy is a mess. You should see him."

The FAA guy responds, "You mean, he can't fly the plane?"

"No, he flies the plane pretty well. But I don't think you should let him fly. You should see him! He's been burned all over his body! His fingers are gone!"

"Can he fly the plane!"

"Yes, yes. He flies the plane fine! But really, you wouldn't believe what he looks like!"

And on and on. Finally, the FAA guy gets through: I can't see this pupil of yours, and furthermore, I don't care how pretty he is. The point is, can he fly?

It's a small scene that illustrates a larger point in life. So often we see things without bothering to look inside.

So I came back to the flying club at ten the next morning. The instructor let me do the preflight routine by myself. As I climbed in, he opened the passenger door. His words were, "Good luck." His face said, "Don't screw up." This was a small and impoverished flying club with only two airplanes; I don't think he was particularly concerned about the pushy, burned-up guy getting killed, but he would have hated like hell to lose that plane. He closed the door and walked away. I was on my own.

I flew like a bird. One more limitation had fallen. One more obstacle had turned into an opportunity.

Each day, I could do more: put on my own boots, open a book, twist a doorknob. While I had, and have, no fingers to speak off, surgeries to loosen the skin in my hands have gradually allowed me to make a good "pinch." The thumb of the left hand had been removed except for a small stump. On the right hand, there was a bit more of my thumb, but in order for it to be useful, they had to remove the index finger completely to make a gap between that and the next digit, to provide the "pinch."

I also made an important discovery about my appearance. If I behaved as if I looked odd—kept my head low, mumbled, refused to meet people's eyes—I was treated as an odd-looking character. But if I behaved in my normal, pre-burn extrovert mode—speaking up, making eye contact, and thrusting out my stump to shake hands as if it were the most normal bit of social intercourse imaginable—people could get beyond my looks literally within seconds and focus on who I was and what I was saying.

The self-development gurus call this "behaving as if," and it's a good idea for anyone. If you want to be attractive, well-liked, in command, happy, try behaving as if you are. There are very few of us who don't have at least a few scars, even if they are only on the inside. But stick with your impersonation of a successful, unscarred person, and you'll find it melts into the core of your personality. You'll be what you wanted to be.

So, I was doing well, but this is not to say I was constantly serene, which brings me to the subject of psychiatric help.

I had seen a few psychiatrists in the hospital. They were sent to me. This is standard procedure for someone in my condition. We had good discussions, but for the most part, they seemed amazed at my ability to cope. I don't recall any intimation that I was crazy, though I was often reminded that it would be quite logical to go nuts in such a situation.

But once out of the hospital, my relationship with Rita began coming unglued—and I was afraid that I was, too. We argued. I had been a cable car gripman, a pilot, a true

San Francisco bohemian who wanted to do it all. Now out of the hospital, the former gripman, the grounded pilot, was a disabled, disfigured caricature of that robust fellow. My always bad temper was now multiplied tenfold. The anger that I felt at being unable to do even simple things all came together at certain moments with Rita.

Added to the stresses and strains of a dissolving relationship was the fact that I had been told, over and over and over again, that it would be quite normal for someone who had undergone this experience to go crazy. Today, understanding as thoroughly as I do that we can make our own choices and there are no absolutes, I would shrug that off. But then it got to me.

Was I crazy?

I checked in with a shrink who had been recommended to me by a doctor. I saw him about five times. Finally, he said, "You know, I am really enjoying these talks, but I have a feeling that there is a question you want to ask me. I think that is why you have come."

He was silent.

I blurted it out.

"Sometimes, I feel crazy. Sometimes, I show incredible rage to the person I should appreciate the most. Sometimes, I have no idea how to handle this situation I find myself in. So many people have told me to expect to go crazy, I thought I would check in with a pro to see if that is what's happening."

He paused.

"I see a lot of people. Some are crazy. Some are normal. I put you in the normal group. I don't know how someone handles your situation, either. But it seems to me you are handling it very well. If you want to come back next week, feel free. But don't come because you think you need to, because you don't. I think you are going to be fine."

That was all I needed to hear.

In fact, ironically, my growing competence and my increasing refusal to accept any limitations turned out to be a problem not in real life—but in the courts.

Chapter 9

"In my youth," said his father, "I took to the law,
And argued each case with my wife;
And the muscular strength which it gave to my jaw
Has lasted the rest of my life."
—Lewis Carroll

I'm told that lawyers began swarming around my hospital room long before I regained consciousness. It's no wonder. This was no stiff-neck-from-whiplash case, and the pain and suffering were abundantly clear. Rita shooed away the ambulance-chasers and got a referral from Blackie, who by then was in his last year of law school. He told her to call Pat Coyle, who was just getting established with a hotshot personal injury attorney named John Brennan. So by the time I knew what was going on, my case was well underway.

I never met Brennan in the hospital, but Coyle came a number of times, not only because this was a lawyer's dream case, but also because he sincerely seemed to care about me and my condition. During the two years between the time I was burned and the time I went to trial, the therapy of having someone to shoot the breeze with—not to mention argue with—helped greatly.

They were convinced we had a good case against both Honda and the company that owned the laundry truck. So we sued them for a total of $2.75 million. That figure was based on the idea that this poor, ruined, hideous heap of flesh (me) would never be able to drive a car, hold a job, do anything but vegetate, and that amount of money would compensate me for a lifetime of lost earnings.

We went to trial in June 1973, two years after the

accident. By then, there was little I could not do, but the lawyers insisted I go out of my way not to look too able. They wanted someone to attend me at all times. I remember going to the men's room in the courthouse alone one time, and as I came out, Coyle saw me and his face became ashen. He practically grabbed me, dragged me to the side of the hallway and demanded, "What in hell do you think you're doing?"

"I had to take a leak," I said.

"Did you realize that one of their lawyers was in there at the same time? From now on, I'll go in with you."

The opposition focused on the fact that I was flying again and seemed to be fairly competent; Brennan and Coyle responded by having a film made of me, highlighting all the things I could not do.

This highlights the strangeness of our legal system, which rewards helplessness and penalizes success. I had no problem with suing. My life had been interrupted, and getting fried was not how I would have chosen to spend that afternoon. What we finally discovered, however, was that it was not my apparent helplessness, but my friendliness and charm that were our greatest legal allies. The jury liked me; I think they even admired me. That, more than anything, made the opposing attorneys eager to settle.

We had a good case against the laundry truck driver, since his story differed from that of the witnesses. He claimed he was on 26th and I smacked him as I crossed on South Van Ness. But even if he were telling the truth, he was in the wrong, as 26th had the stop sign, and South Van Ness didn't.

The suit against Honda was a tougher nut. Honda crashed thirteen motorcycles—all of which were loaded with sandbags to simulate a human rider—into a concrete wall, and could not make the gas cap come open. In the courtroom, they brought in a similar tank and beat on it with a rubber mallet. The cap stayed on. There was a lot of high theater in this case: Honda's lawyer would make some point and punctuate it with a WHACK! on the tank. Honda had no end of expert witnesses testifying that it was impossible for the cap to open in a crash.

But we went to our own independent testing laboratory in Colorado. The white-suit guys there determined that a human body moving across the cap, as would happen in a front-on collision, could open it. In fact, a few years later, I met a guy in the hospital who had been badly burned in a similar way on a Honda 750. He got $450,000, thanks to Pat Coyle, from the company.

But the clearest evidence confirming that the gas cap had popped open emerged when Coyle questioned the first police officer to arrive on the scene. The officer made it abundantly clear that no one had tampered with the motorcycle, because it was still red-hot and smoking when he arrived, and the crowd was standing back in a ring thirty feet in diameter. The gas cap, which was hinged to the tank, was popped open, and there was only one way in the world that could have happened—the forward motion of my body across the cap had defeated the "foolproof" cap-locking mechanism.

So, two weeks into the trial, the judge decided there should be a settlement conference. He feared extremes: I would either get no money or too much money, either of which would lead to endless appeals.

So, after this conference, my lawyers gave me the news. The defendants had offered $450,000 apiece. My share of the $900,000, after the lawyer's fees, would be about $500,000. I had to decide: should I shoot craps and go for more, with a chance of getting nothing, or should I take the offer?

That's a big decision. But from the start, I had decided that this was "found" money. I knew my life was okay, and it seemed pointless to get greedy.

I took the money.

One final note on the psychiatric front. Around the time of my trial, my lawyers could not believe that I was not seeing a shrink, so they got me one.

If ever anyone *needed* a shrink, it was this guy. He had serious psychological problems, most notably a god-complex. He was convinced he had all the answers and his therapy-group participants knew nothing. Several group members had bought into this charade; there were a bunch of people who had been seeing this nutcase for four years, convinced they could not survive without his omniscience. These people were clearly addicted to the idea that they were sick.

I agree that psychiatry has its place and some people have scars that are so deep that they need more than a Swedish massage. But I could not understand this brand of group therapy at all. Sure, sometimes things don't feel good, you get pissed off, nobody likes you... to which my reaction is, welcome aboard, nice to have you here on Spaceship Earth. You can spend your whole life focusing on the worst aspects of your life if you choose to. Do you want to spend all of your time focusing on how bad your relationship, job, appearance is, or do you want to focus on how good it can become? Do you want to talk only about how bad smoking is, or shall we focus on how wonderful fresh air and health can be? The idea of self-help groups should be just that—to help people understand that the decision is up to them. As I see it, you can also sleep on a bed of nails and wallop your forehead every half-hour with a two-by-four if that's your desire. But wallowing in angst is not my thing, and that's what these sessions were all about.

So after a few sessions, I quit. I pointed out that I did not want to spend an hour a week thinking about problems that I considered to be relatively minor, when there was so much positive stuff to do and be in the world. I even threw them some Morehouse—the idea that we are all perfect—because, while I resisted that idea for quite a while, it does make some sense.

I got a lot of major-league hostility from the group, but what stands out is a letter I got from the shrink. The gist was, sure, now, in 1973, I was doing well, but if I did not get long-term therapy, sooner or later I would jump out a window.

I haven't jumped.

Chapter 10

Never does nature say one thing and wisdom another.
—Juvenal

It was at this time, the spring of 1973, that I had my post-burn epiphany.

Rita and I took a vacation to Hawaii, bumming around the outer islands. Finally, on a visit to the big island, Hawaii, we were relaxing on a blanket on a deserted, postcard-pretty, white-sand beach at Kealakekua, and the notion came upon me to swim.

I did not own a bathing suit; I did not think I could swim. My left elbow did not, and does not, bend (after being crushed in the motorcycle crash, it was immobilized by a metal plate screwed to the bones, and to this day has only about a ten-degree range of motion). I had no fingers, my skin was still tight—and the list goes on. The shallow end of the YMCA pool, with two lifeguards, a physical therapist, and perhaps a couple of lawyers in attendance was a likely place for me to resume swimming. This place we were had waves as tall as I was.

But what the hell!

I took off all of my clothes and, trailed by John Kupihea, a friend who was convinced I would drown, strode into the waves.

I swam and bodysurfed like a porpoise.

I call that my rebirth, my second baptism.

I really knew, at that moment, that there was nothing that I could not do.

I had conquered my last limitation. I still could not do buttons—I still, I suppose, could not be one hundred percent independent—but psychologically, I was one hundred percent. I had finished the cycle of being burned.

It's significant that this moment occurred in a natural setting, rather than, say, a church. I am not a particularly religious person. I am not an atheist, but neither do I pretend to have any real knowledge of what's behind the universe. Many people have told me that (a) I must be a terrible person and my misfortunes show I am being punished for my sins; or (b) I am a saint here to show the world how to rise above limitations of the flesh. I like "b" better, but the fact remains: I don't know. Sometimes, after my speeches, people ask me what role God or Christ played in my recovery. I explain to them that a number of people around me, including Rita's grandmother, prayed fervently for me, and I have no doubt those prayers made a difference. But I add that those prayers were based on love and caring, and I'm not sure which deity, if any, interceded on my behalf.

This attitude upsets some people, but as long as there are 52,000 known religions on earth, many of which contradict each other, and I'm one little guy with no direct pipeline to the infinite, I'm sticking with my "religion": I believe in the healing power of love, but beyond that, I don't know.

Nonetheless, touching bases with eternity, as I had in that accident, awakened in me a new desire: to cut through the chaff of life and find what lay at its base, what was real. Back when I was in that hospital bed with my eyelids sewn shut, I would have June Fulbright read to me from *In Wildness is the Preservation of the World*, with text by Henry David Thoreau and photos by Elliot Porter. As people read to me, the pictures appeared in my brain, and I could focus on the beauty of the natural world rather than the limitations of my own situation.

I had long been an outdoors type, but for me, a mountain was primarily a place to ski down, a river was fun to run on a raft, and both were prettier places to have a party than the average urban condo.

Right after I got out of the hospital, I immediately tried skiing again, (remember: don't be afraid to try the hard stuff *first*) but I must admit it was a bit of a disaster.

Skiing is equipment-intensive anyway, and with no fingers to manipulate the infinite number of snaps, zippers, and clamps, and with my typical impatience, Rita was put out with me. This difficult trip to Badger Pass in Yosemite was one of a series of strains and another signal that Rita would stay with me only as long as it took me to regain my independence. (Incidentally, later, in Colorado, I became an excellent skier. Rather than using elaborate macramé to lash the poles to my hands, I just skipped the poles altogether.)

But soon after that, I tried a new way of experiencing the wilderness, one that was truer to the sense of the Thoreau book. I just looked at it.

After we returned from Hawaii, I spent a great deal of time around Yosemite. One reason, I'm sure, was that I did not have to explain to the owls and deer how I had been burned. Another was that the exercise of hiking speeded my recuperation.

But the main reason was that I felt a sudden, profound, overwhelming connection with the natural, unbuilt, untouched, unspoiled world. Having been burned back nearly to an elemental state, I felt a new disdain for the ugly, man-made environment that was rapaciously consuming the planet. I wanted to go back. I wanted to know the roots, where I came from.

Soon, I felt that just visiting natural places was not enough. I wanted to live in one.

Crested Butte, Colorado, is an old coal-mining town nestled at an altitude of 8,885 feet in a sparsely populated valley. It's twenty-five miles as the Cessna flies from Aspen, but 217 miles by paved roads, which illustrates its remoteness. The interstate does not even come near it. It is at the end of a twenty-eight-mile-long paved road that veers off Federal Highway 50, which is itself sparsely used. Its heyday was the 1920s. It went bust in 1952 when the mine shut down. In 1973, it had perhaps six hundred year-round residents, mostly well-educated urban dropouts who came there to ski, along with a sprinkling of old miners. It was a town most of the world had passed by.

That suited me.

It was stunningly beautiful. It had soaring, snowy peaks around it, including its namesake, Crested Butte Mountain, which sits in the middle of the East River Valley. It is called Crested Butte because it stands alone, unattached to the other mountains. It's twelve thousand feet high, while the mountains around it are over thirteen thousand feet. Because these proved to have in them very little in the way of precious metals—though God knows, gold and silver miners had looked for them—these mountains remained unspoiled and were later set aside as wilderness areas by Congress. The national forests around Crested Butte constitute one of America's most beautiful back yards.

And the town itself was nearly as striking as its surrounding scenery. It was full of western Victorian houses, small but charming houses, built by coal miners. Miles Rademan, Crested Butte's town planner, said, "While the rest of America was apologizing for its past, Crested Butte slept. It was too poor to tear down its historic buildings and cover the rest with aluminum siding."

So by the time the urban dropouts arrived in the 1970s, the preservation ethic was in full swing, and they worked to maintain and improve the town's historic character rather than to modernize it. The result is a slice of the Old West; not the touristy version, but the real thing.

And Crested Butte filled other needs I had. I was growing tired of the stares, the questions. In a big city, where one is always coming into contact with new people, relationships tend to be shallow, based on obvious roles and characteristics. Too often, people were dealing with me as "the burned guy."

In a little town, I figured within a few weeks everyone would learn the story of how it happened, get past my weird face, and begin dealing with me as a person. I also wanted to live somewhere beautiful, quiet, yet easily accessible by air, and with good business prospects.

Crested Butte, it turned out, provided all of the above.

I bought a house, one of the nicest in town that had been built in 1886. I became part-owner of a huge, commercial building called "The Company Store," because, back in the mining days, it really was the company store. Soon, a bar on the premises called "The Tailings" went belly-up; I took it over and found I could tend bar better with no fingers than most people could with a full set. I bought a few house lots which promptly tripled in value, built a huge, log building with apartments in it, and generally became a successful entrepreneur.

It wasn't hard. The area was booming. Aspen was ridiculously overpriced, and more and more fed-up urbanites began flocking to sleepy, forgotten, and cheap towns nestled in equally lovely parts of the Rockies, either to vacation or live. Crested Butte was one of them.

Somewhere in here, my relationship with Rita skidded to a stop. All along, she had stuck by me and done everything for me. Because of her great heart and generosity of spirit, I think she would have gladly buttoned my buttons and tied my shoes forever, but what she finally could not abide was being my lightening rod, the ground for my high-voltage outbursts when life became too frustrating.

She left. I was completely on my own.

Then came the luckiest business deal of my life. Eager to pick up a 1939 Cadillac in New Hampshire (I adored it and had spent a year getting the owner to part with it), I hitched a ride with Murray Howell, a free spirit, beer-aholic, and visionary, who was one of my business partners in Crested Butte. While chucking empties into the back seat of the station wagon (by the time we arrived, it was full to the roof, and I confess I contributed my share), he explained that his brother-in-law Duncan Syme, whom he portrayed as a sort of mad-scientist inventor tinkering in a barn in Warren, Vermont, had an idea for a woodstove that looked promising. I thought Murray was nuts, though as we drove along, he pointed out the long lines at the gas stations (this was the middle of the energy crisis). Eventually, he convinced me to mail ahead one thousand dollars so that Syme could keep tinkering as we approached.

I will never forget the weekend of July 4, 1975. Syme, a small guy with wire-rim glasses who looked like a cross between a mad scientist and a hippy, lived with his family in a barn on some property he was renting. It was an extraordinarily hot day, and Syme trotted out a rectangular iron box, crudely welded and wired together, with what seemed a Rube-Goldberg collection of vents, pipes, and dampers hanging off it. Syme explained that this stove was different from any made in America. Where Franklin stoves were lucky to achieve five percent efficiency, this stove—with its secondary combustion chamber and airtight fire-box—was over forty-seven percent efficient.

His spiel was persuasive, but what really impressed me was that, with just a small fire inside it, it was about 150 degrees anywhere within two hundred feet of this box. With no further ado, I invested twenty-four thousand dollars in the company. I asked Syme and his team to make me chairman of the board; I figured if this venture did fly, it would look good on my résumé; and I did have some good experience to contribute. These guys were inventors, not businessmen, and this company would need all the help it could get.

Soon, they came back for more. My financial advisor thought I was an idiot, and I was tempted to agree with him. But eventually, I invested some sixty-five thousand dollars.

I did it all on gut feeling, and it was the smartest move, financially, I've ever made. As the energy crisis continued to intensify, the company could barely keep up with demand. It became the second largest private employer in the state of Vermont, with dealerships in all fifty states (yes, even Hawaii). My life was far better than it had been before I was burned. Suddenly, I was a millionaire.

The lesson? How many things do we say no to because they are not guaranteed? How many of us are not willing to risk our time, energy, or money for success? The idea of being a risk-taker applies to more than just financial wealth. It applies to emotional wealth as well. Many people ask for sure things, and wind up with no things.

Almost everyone who has become a great success in our society has been willing to take risks, and when they failed, were willing to try again, and again, and again.

They must have had Billy glued to the pedestal to take this one.
Credit: W Mitchell Collection

Camp Sesquehawe,
summer 1949.
Credit: W Mitchell Collection

School days—algebra was a total loss.
Inset: Naval camp was great fun. It was
there that Mitchell learned to sail.
Credit: W Mitchell Collection

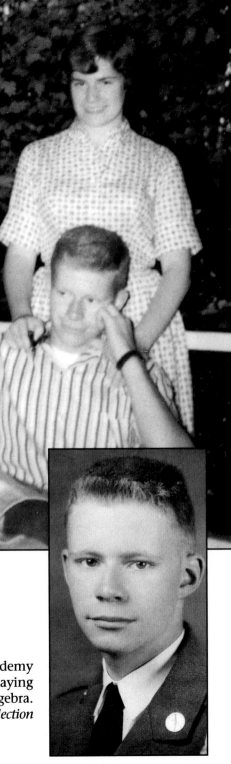

Mitchell and his two sisters, Karen and
Gretchen. *Credit: W Mitchell Collection*

At 15, a cadet at Augusta Military Academy
in Virginia. Mitchell specialized in playing
the tuba and not learning algebra.
Credit: W Mitchell Collection

Mitchell and Annie in the traditional campaign photo.
Credit: Bob Brazell Photography

Annie was a tireless campaigner. If there had been two of her, we could have won. (Hannibel helped, too.)
Credit: Paul Gallaher Photography

A brief visit home during the
1984 congressional race.
Credit: Paul Gallaher Photography

So many people worked so very
hard. And they had fun, too.
Credit: W Mitchell Collection

Kathy Joyce congratulates Mitchell upon winning the impossible primary in 1984.
Credit: Paul Gallaher Photography

Myles Rademan (center, standing) was a guide, a friend, and "the brains of the outfit" in our battle with Amax.
Credit: Paul Gallaher Photography

The beginning of one more remarkable journey was the race for mayor of Crested Butte. *Credit: Paul Gallaher Photography*

Hannibel, his daughter, Hana, Annie, and Mitchell.
Credit: W Mitchell Collection

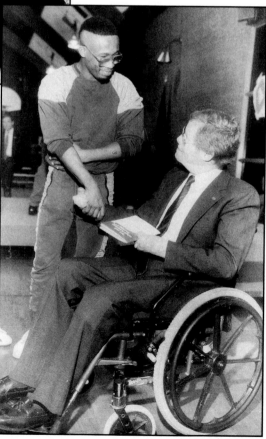

Meeting people who have been given special challenges (as in this training center for people with development disabilities) reminds Mitchell of our responsibility to our entire family.
Credit: Johnstown Tribune-Democrat

Mitchell continues his love for flying in Australia in his friend, Max Hitchen's plane. *Credit: W Mitchell Collection*

Sky diving helped Mitchell continue to break the bonds of conventional thinking. *Credit: W Mitchell Collection*

The first time Mitchell met President Carter, he literally bumped into him in a White House hallway. *Credit: Official White House Photo*

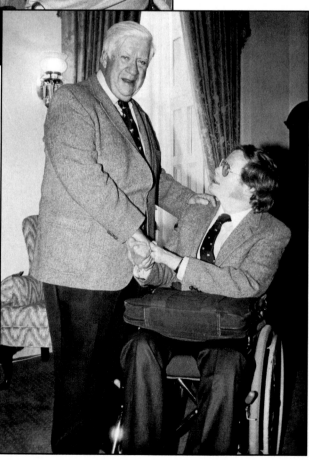

You need lots of friends to save a mountain and a town. It helps to start at the top. Tip O'Neill, former Speaker of the U.S. House of Representatives. *Credit: W Mitchell Collection*

Lee and Gary Hart. Gary Hart was one of the brightest people in public service. Very few understood how much America lost by his leaving politics. *Credit: Paula Haikara*

Geraldine Ferraro, the first major party VP candidate to be a woman. *Credit: W Mitchell Collection*

Senator Paul Simon (third from left), 1984. *Credit: W Mitchell Collection*

Jim Wright, former Speaker of the House of Representatives, made a small mistake and paid the big price of being forced to resign from office. *Credit: W Mitchell Collection*

Mitchell's mother's favorite photo from his public life—Mr. and Mrs. Cary Grant (1987). *Credit: W Mitchell Collection*

Marge Schott, owner of the Cincinnati Reds, whose compassion for the underpriviledged didn't get any headlines. *Credit: W Mitchell Collection*

The only thing better than speaking to an audience is speaking to an audience in Hawaii—in this case 1,200 people at a Tony Robbins seminar—August 1989.
Credit: Harry Knobel

The sky's the limit—there's almost nothing we can't do.
Credit: JJ Jowdy Photography

Yes, I'm friends with Marilyn Monroe. She is the executive vice president of the Texas Society of Association Executives.
Credit: JJ Jowdy Photography

AT&T was so moved by Mitchell's story that they created a "Star Fish" award for the employee who makes the biggest difference to a co-worker.
Credit: Allan's Photography

The "Eyes of Texas" were upon Mitchell at Corpus Christi in 1989.
Credit: JJ Jowdy Photography

Chapter 11

Adversity reveals genius.
—Horace

Life had come full circle for me. I had accomplished a great deal since I had been hauled, smoking, out of that fiery intersection. Along with my business successes, I had pursued flying with a passion; and now I had commercial, multi-engine, and instrument ratings. I literally felt that I was unstoppable.

I bought a Cessna 206. The plane was dubbed "the station wagon of airplanes" because of its cargo-capacity and overall safety. I used every excuse I could to take it out. On one particular day, November 11, 1975, I was heading to San Francisco to visit friends.

To save money—even millionaires can go broke with a hobby like flying—and for companionship, I often ran a classified ad offering to fly passengers to wherever I happened to be headed in exchange for fuel money. Four guys signed on. One, Tim Rolf, I knew; he was also a pilot and had made this trip with me before. The other three were strangers.

That morning was the most beautiful you can imagine: clear, calm, and cold, about fifteen degrees. Gunnison Airport, which is about twenty-eight miles south of Crested Butte, had no heated hangars, and most planes, including mine, were stored outside. It had rained and snowed in the two weeks since I had flown the plane, and about half an inch of ice and crusty snow had accumulated on the wings.

One of the cardinal rules of flying is to never take off with ice on the wings. So we turned the plane so that the sun shone on the surface of the wings. Then, with brooms and ice scrapers, we dislodged as much ice as we could. We agreed to go have breakfast in town, to give the plane an hour in the sun to melt the ice. When we came back, we scraped and brushed some more, to the point that I honestly believed we had removed it all. It was not until the FAA report came out weeks later that I learned there was still a quarter of an inch of ice left on the wings when we took off.

We taxied and filled up. We had a full load. The plane was supposed to be able to take six people and fifty pounds of luggage. We had five people and more than fifty pounds of gear. I guessed we were about fifty pounds under the limit, but we were certainly close.

I wanted to gain a flight instructor's rating, so I suggested that Tim sit in the left seat, where the pilot generally sits, and do the takeoff, and I would take the right seat, where the instructor would normally sit. You can fly from either position, as there are dual controls, and I had flown from the right seat a number of times.

He started the takeoff roll. When we got one-third of the way down the runway, I did not like the sound of the engine. He chopped the power on my instruction, we taxied back and ran the engine up to one hundred percent. Everything seemed fine.

I was skittish because I had been having trouble with the plane during the previous month. On a trip from Denver, I had suffered a severe power loss and was sure I would crash. But it turned out that a mechanic had failed to properly connect the hose to the turbocharger, the device that forces air into the engine to allow it to run well at high altitudes. A week after that, I had chopped power on takeoff at the Grand Canyon and discovered a hunk of hose carelessly left inside the turbocharger, blocking the airflow.

With these worries in mind, I suggested that I had better handle the takeoff. I had almost a thousand hours of flight time compared to Tim's two hundred.

So we took off. We got up to one hundred feet.

I was thinking very hard.

The plane was not reacting the way I thought it should; it seemed sluggish, unresponsive. In that second, I had to decide what to do. I still had runway left. I decided to reduce the power and land the plane again.

When I pulled back on the throttle, the plane stalled.

"Stall" means that even though the engine is still running, the wings are no longer "flying," because air is not passing around them quickly enough to provide lift.

I screamed "Hang on!"

We dropped for an endless two seconds and slammed like a rock back onto the runway and landed flat, pancaked, with a tremendous jolt, breaking one of the landing gear.

The busted gear made the plane tilt to the right. That caused gasoline from the just-filled, forty-three-gallon tanks to spill out of the overflow vents and across the wing. This is not normally dangerous, but I had a more detailed knowledge than most of what gas leaking out of a crashed vehicle can do. I killed the power and turned off the electrical switches.

"Get out!" I barked at the guys. "Everyone out! Now!"

They got out. I couldn't.

At first, I did not realize what had happened. I tried two or three times to get out, and concluded that my feet must be stuck under the rudder pedals.

It was only after that that I noted the numbness in my legs and the ache in my back. As the moments passed, the pain became intense.

I could not move my legs.

A fire engine and an ambulance pulled up within five minutes, though it felt like a lifetime. There was never a fire, thank God. I told the paramedics about my condition and they pulled me, very carefully, out of the plane by unhooking the entire seat, then gingerly transferring me to a back-support board.

At Gunnison Valley Hospital, Dr. John Tarr, a ski buddy and a close friend, examined me and knew immediately that my numb legs were not a good sign. John and the other emergency-room workers were all friends and acquaintances of mine. They had to know, as medical experts, that there was a damn good chance this was not fixable. I still remember the look on John's face. I had never seen him look so serious, so compassionate—so shaken. He called an air ambulance—ironically, it was another Cessna 206—and it flew me to St. Anthony's, a trauma center in Denver.

I was paralyzed. For the next two days, they did every test you can imagine on me. During this period, I learned that two of my passengers had gone to a hospital but were released right away; one of them went dancing that night. Rolf and the fourth passenger were being held for observation for a few days, and though they had to wear back braces for a time, both were performing routine duties as ski patrolmen later that winter.

Meantime, preliminary examination revealed that my paralysis was complete—there was no feeling, no motor function. An X-ray showed the twelfth thoracic vertebrae, at the base of my spine, was crushed.

But I wanted to know exactly what had happened. So I gave consent—against the advice of several of my doctor friends—for a laminectomy, an operation in which the doctors open up the cartilage in the spine and actually look inside. The possible gain in knowledge is counterbalanced by the risk that the operation itself could damage the cord.

The operation went well. It revealed that my cord looked perfectly healthy.

So why was I paralyzed? Because, though there was no visible sign of it, the cord had apparently been bruised. As it was described to me, the amount of pressure needed to permanently injure the cord is about the same as your buddy gently punching you in the arm. On your arm, that gentle punch makes a light bruise because of dead blood cells that are quickly removed and replaced with healthy cells. The spinal cord does not work that way. Dead spinal cord cells can't regenerate.

But there are mysteries surrounding the spinal cord that no one has fathomed. Dr. Robert Jackson, my primary physician, told me that sometimes, a spinal cord can look like "hamburger" and, despite the damage, can still work to some degree. Conversely, a perfect-looking cord like mine can be nonfunctional. Unfortunately, I seemed to fall into the latter category.

On the morning of the third day of tests, Dr. Jackson came in. By this point I had been moved out of St. Anthony's and into Craig Hospital, which specialized in long-term rehabilitative care.

Jackson was a big guy, with an authoritative manner. He clearly saw no point in drawing out this announcement.

"Mitchell," he said, "it appears that you will never walk again. It appears you'll have to use a wheelchair for the rest of your life."

It was quiet in the room.

Then it all caught up with me.

Outwardly, I maintained my poise. To this day, I don't recall exactly what I said. It may well have been nothing, or it might have even been a wisecrack, along the lines of the "This'll destroy my pool game" remark I had made when I found I was sans fingers.

But inside, I was devastated.

It was the most incredible of the incredible.

I had spent four years recovering from the most devastating injury a human being can incur and live. It had been the battle of a lifetime, and I had won it. If anyone deserved smooth sailing for the rest of his life, I was the guy.

It simply seemed to be too much for one person to bear.

I lay in that bed.

I wondered if there was anything left of my life.

Why me? No one had an answer to that one.

But now I had little time to mope. My support system was far bigger than it had been when I was burned. Literally hundreds of folks from Crested Butte made the five-hour drive to see me. They came just to tell me they cared, just to encourage me. I came to see, more than ever before, how friendships are "investments" that offer protection in a crisis that no insurance policy can give.

One day, a young woman from Crested Butte called me. She said, "Mitchell, I don't even know if you remember this. But a year ago, when I was going through a really rough time, you said something to me that I will never forget. You told me that, 'It's not what happens to you. It's what you do about it.' Do you still believe that, Mitchell?"

I thought about that. It's tough when your own pontificating comes back to haunt you.

But maybe I had known what I was talking about. Being burned to a crisp had not ruined my life. In many ways, it had made me grow, change, improve in ways of which I could not have dreamed.

If there was no absolute relationship between being burned and being miserable, then it followed that there was no absolute link between being paralyzed and being doubly miserable. This experience would be what I made of it, not what others thought I should make of it.

Taking charge had literally saved my life after I was burned. I decided to take charge again.

Unlike my experience four years earlier, I was fully conscious and, at least from the navel up, completely healthy.

I got busy. I decided on a three-part strategy:

First, I would not rule out the possibility that I might recover. There are cases in which paralysis is only temporary. But of those few people who recover, most do so within days, fewer within weeks, almost no one within months. As the days dragged on, I knew that the chance was only one in a million, or one in ten million. But countless lottery tickets are sold on the basis of odds longer than that.

There are no absolutes in the world.

If you build a barricade of absolutes, even likely pieces of happiness can be walled out. Much more so the unlikely pieces.

Second, I would, at the same time, do the work

necessary to prepare for a lifetime of paralysis. I would learn to use the wheelchair, to deal with the unpredictable bowel and bladder activity that accompanies this condition. Many young people who are paralyzed insist that they *will* recover, they *will* walk, so it is pointless to gain such skills. This is denial and does no one any good. Lying in bed wishing for recovery simply atrophies muscles, angers therapists, and boosts already astronomical hospital bills.

Third, I would take the best counsel I could get, but I would make the decisions. By now, I was a firm believer in control, and its role in a healthy life. No one would do anything to me unless they had explained the need for it and I had agreed.

Chapter 12

Destiny is not a matter of chance; it is a matter of choice.
It is not a thing to be waited for; it is a thing to be achieved.
—William Jennings Bryan

It's funny how people behave in hospitals. Corporate executives, drill sergeants, mothers—people accustomed to being in command—often go limp in hospitals. Worse, fun people, folks who are normally the life of the party, become somber, quiet, sterile, the better to fit into the somber, quiet, sterile surroundings.

Well, to hell with that. The way I see it, doctors and nurses are your friends at best, your paid advisors at worst, but it is nowhere written that they are your dictators. Immediately after my transfer to Craig Hospital, where my rehabilitation work would be done, I instituted a few changes:

First, every afternoon at 4:30, I had ice delivered to my room to chill the beer and champagne for "happy hour." It was a daily party for patients, particularly Bob Rosner and Herb Darling, who along with me were at least ten years older than the average spinal-cord patient. Bob had broken his neck diving into shallow water in the Caribbean (take it from Bob: drinking and diving is at least as dangerous as drinking and driving). Herb had fallen from a deer-hunting platform in a tree. The room soon became a popular hangout for other patients and the free spirits among the nursing staff.

I also began what I called "businessmen's lunches." There were two hundred other paralysis patients at Craig. The typical one was young, male, and utterly devastated because he had done it to himself by acting stupid—driving drunk, diving into shallow water, trying an idiotic stunt while skiing. Today, when I talk to audiences, I mention that the overwhelming majority of spinal-cord injuries occur because some people still don't use seat belts. It is a three-second insurance policy that many a patient at Craig Hospital dearly wishes he had taken out.

Anyway, at age thirty-two, I was older than most of them and became a sort of godfather to the ward. I used to order an "ambo" cab—one with a lift to transport wheelchairs—and take a few of them at a time to a seedy Mexican restaurant down on Larimer Street. Just the change in atmosphere wrought an amazing change in all of us. We stopped talking about the paralysis, about our problems, about how difficult our life ahead would probably be. We had a chance there to tell bad jokes, eyeball the local female talent, and generally behave like normal, healthy, American males. After several visits, the management even got used to all of that wheelchair chrome.

The only problem was that, when you are a paraplegic, you don't get feedback from your bowels. Spicy food, along with the relaxing effect of a couple or six margaritas, makes this unpredictable situation even more so. So the nurses complained about having to clean up after these guys and that they often came back too relaxed to do their physical therapy. But, important as P.T. is, there are other kinds of therapy that matter more. Being normal means more than learning to pilot a wheelchair. These young guys were party animals, and going out on the town to drink and carouse was what they needed.

The height of my rehabilitation program was on Super Bowl Sunday, when I arranged a full, catered buffet in my room. To make the celebration really zip, I figured we should have some Everclear punch. For those who have never had the pleasure of tasting Everclear, it is 180-proof grain alcohol. Sprayed from an atomizer, it also makes a great bug killer. My point of view was anything that pure had to be good for you, but the nurses put their foot down on that one, as it would not mix well with some of the medications the guys were taking.

We made do with less intimidating beverages, and a good time was had by all.

Hospitals should make this kind of stuff easy; but, in fact, I had to fight mighty battles for privileges that are taken for granted in the real world. When I first became a patient, my most vociferous assaults were launched at one particular R.N. I nicknamed "Nurse Ratchet," after the domineering ward supervisor in Ken Kesey's novel *One Flew Over the Cuckoo's Nest.*

For example, there was the battle of the telephone system. When this second accident had occurred, I was quite a successful businessman with interests and investments all across the nation. On a normal day, I made perhaps thirty telephone calls, and I had no intention of changing that. The insistence on rest and quiet in hospitals is often just an invitation for the patient to worry about his awful fate. I chose to get on with my life.

The hospital's telephone system required every call to go through an overworked operator, and it shut down completely at 8 p.m. It was adequate for chatting with one's wife about how the kids are doing in school. It was a disaster for someone with needs like mine.

The battle became World War III one night when I wanted to be turned. Paraplegics are turned periodically to ease their discomfort, and I was in pain. I asked, nicely, to be turned sooner than my schedule said I should. Ratchet refused.

I asked more forcefully.

No go.

I demanded.

No.

I said, "Call my doctor, have him write some new orders."

"It's too late," she said.

"It's not too late for me," I said, "He's my doctor, I am paying his bill. Give me the phone.

"It's nine," she said sweetly. "The switchboard for the patients' phones closes at eight."

That was a moment of incredible frustration. I'm

paralyzed, I'm in quite serious pain, I can't get the phone, I can't get turned, I can't even get a damned aspirin.

So I plotted.

The next morning, the doctor came to see me on his usual rounds.

I was very cordial.

"Good morning," I said. "I am curious. You were unavailable to treat me last night. Who is my doctor at night?"

He assured me that he was always my doctor, day and night.

"When I asked the nurse to contact you, she would not do it, and I could not call on the phone myself. I had no physician last night."

I went on, tossing out the term "malpractice" once or twice, just to be sure I had his attention. I am sure, had she called him the night before, he would have given her grief. But after our talk, I actually became the first patient in the history of that hospital to have a private, outside line strung into his room at my request, and at my expense, of course. Nurse Ratchet became a lot more accommodating.

But the true test of normalcy, for me, was trying my luck with the ladies. My physical therapist, Beverly, and I became particularly close. After lying on my back for a month to let my spine heal, it then became necessary for me to do stretches: my favorite involved Beverly sitting behind me and pushing me forward. Man, I could have done that one all day.

I remember that one wheelchair skill she was trying to teach me was getting out of the chair and onto a couch. I was tired and cranky that day. I'd already spent a lot of time learning wheelchair-to-car, wheelchair-to-toilet, and so on. And a couch, being lower, looked like too much work. I told her so.

"Look," she said, "when you are in a wheelchair, there are only two ways to get close to a woman. One is in bed, which, depending on the woman, can take some time. The other is on a couch. So think about that."

Suddenly, I was incredibly motivated. I became the all-time hospital champion at wheelchair-to-couch.

But my favorite among the hospital staff was Annie Baker, a beginning nurse who came into my room with great trepidation. I had experienced a streak of bad luck that winter extending beyond the accident. A friend who was living in my house accidentally overloaded the coal stove, which superheated the chimney and burned off the house's entire top floor. And my attorney and good friend, John Brennan, had died unexpectedly of a heart attack.

So when Annie was informed that she would tend a guy who was first burned, now paralyzed, and apparently beset by disaster at every turn, she was understandably prepared for the worst.

But we became friends immediately. She was cute and quite young, eighteen years old. And she warmed to me. After tending people in deepest misery, here was a guy who was always calling for more ice and flirting with everyone around. But I soon learned that she was not easily impressed; she was very self-sufficient. That, more than anything, was to lead me to spend the next few years pursuing her romantically.

In sharp contrast to me was another paralyzed patient, a guy about nineteen years old who retained only partial use of his arms. He had been an extraordinary athlete and an outdoors person; he had climbed mountains, skied, done it all. While I rolled ahead with my busy, romantic, executive life, he was always stone-faced. He grimly performed his rehabilitation exercises, but I never once saw him smile, much less laugh.

That's understandable. No one gets a charge out of being paralyzed, and I had my share of frustrations, too. But I had tried to talk to him, and he would not listen. He was shutting down, and that is not a good sign.

Finally, one day in the gym, I rolled over to him.

"Before all of this happened to me," I said, "there were ten thousand things I could do. Now, there are nine thousand. Sure, I could dwell on the one thousand that I can't do. But I prefer to think about the nine thousand that are left."

It's advice that applies to everyone. For all of the things we cannot do because we're not gorgeous, rich, or adored, there are infinitely more things waiting for us to do, most of which we've never even considered, far more than you could do in a thousand lifetimes. If, in one lifetime, you did five hundred of them, you'd be an Edison, an Einstein.

I would like to report that this exalted wisdom I graciously bestowed upon him instantly changed his life. I think perhaps it did give him a small boost, and sometimes that is all it takes. So often, we do nothing because we feel that we cannot do enough. That's the greatest fallacy in life, because the big things are, in fact, usually a series of little things.

But, perhaps more importantly, it helped me to crystallize the message I have since shared with millions. That bit of advice about "the nine thousand things" is my legacy. It's pinned on walls, it's in a video program that was produced for rehabilitation units all over the country, it is a slogan for the Craig Hospital foundation. Sometimes, it is even more important for the families to hear it, because they can be more devastated than the patients. (Families see few possibilities for the person they love, because the situation has not been thrust on them personally, and they are not the ones who must deal with it.) And I am proud of it, because it is true.

One of my personal "nine thousand things" was continuing to redefine the doctor-patient relationship. After three months in the hospital, I released myself.

Again, the passive tense—"I was released"—is the common one in hospitals, but that attitude smacks of jail to me. Who the hell sentenced me to the hospital? I felt I had recovered enough, and there were things to do back home.

So, at the regular meeting between doctors, nurses, and physical therapists where the progress of each patient is discussed, I pointedly put myself at the head of the table, in the doctor's usual position, in front of my records.

When he came in, he was surprised. I explained to him that I would be in charge of the meeting that day, because I was going home next week.

Confronted with this apparent "coup," he was bemused.

"I'm glad you think you are," he said.

He went around the table, asking if those present thought I should be discharged. They gave nonspecific answers. When he came to Beverly, though, he got the right answer.

"The issue is not whether he should go. I know Mitchell, and if he says he's going, then he is. Perhaps what we should focus on is not whether he should or should not go, but how we can best prepare him in these remaining days for when he gets home."

So they did, and I discharged myself.

Chapter 13

*The sun, the moon, and the stars would have
disappeared long ago, had they happened to be within
the reach of predatory human hands.*
—Havelock Ellis

Although I love it, I have often called Crested Butte "the least wheelchair-accessible town in America," and with 200 inches of snow on the ground when I got home, it was particularly dicey getting around.

But what was particularly glorious was that some carpenter friends of mine, organized and led by John Benjamin, one of the most eccentric, scruffy, and genuinely human people I have ever loved, had chainsawed off the whole burned top floor of my house and replaced it in subzero weather. They had also redone the inside, and the result was far lovelier than the old place had ever been.

So, I was back. While parts of life were good, there were multiple frustrations. The old freedom I'd had to ski when I felt like it, carry in wood, shovel the walk, and be completely independent, was no longer available.

But the friends were still there, and they helped to reduce the frustration.

And there was lots to do. My bar kept me busy, I built another commercial building, and tried to help steer Vermont Castings through a period of astounding growth.

I bought myself a motorhome and had another friend, Gordon Roberts, outfit it for me (after he learned that I had broken my back, he left school in San Francisco and hitchhiked to Denver to be with me in the hospital, simply because he was a friend and wanted to help me). Another friend, Norm Johnson, a theoretical physicist and a former

NASA employee, installed a video and sound system in it that was only slightly less powerful and sophisticated than something one might find on the space shuttle. This mobile den of debauchery became widely known as "Mitchell's Hotel," and was the scene of good times and general bacchanalia.

My long-term plan, such as it was, was to become a vagabond, tooling to Arizona in the winter, returning to Crested Butte in the summer, going wherever the winds blew and the mood struck in the meantime. I called Annie often, inviting her on various expeditions with me. She was cool and casual: she was busy, but perhaps sometime...

Within six months of returning, I flew again with a friend, just to see if I was afraid. I wasn't. It wasn't the airplane that had bit me, after all, but my poor judgment. My first flight was emotional, and short; it was with my friend and lawyer, David Liensdorf. We went only from Crested Butte to Gunnison, a simple 30-mile hop. At Gunnison, we were going to sign some papers to transfer my airplane to a salvage company that had come to collect it. Even though it looked fairly normal except for the smashed propeller and bent landing gear, a plane that had sustained a crash great enough to fracture a spinal column had been too stressed to ever again be airworthy.

I did not get out of David's plane when we pulled up in front of mine. Instead, I found myself caught in a sudden rush of "What ifs?" What if I had just inspected the plane a little more carefully? What if I had decided to boost power and circle back?

Aside from such purposeless musings, there were positive memories that were overwhelming. I had flown so many miles in that plane. I had zoomed over Niagara Falls, circled the Statue of Liberty, skimmed the Florida seashore, and soared over the chasms of Yosemite, and the Grand Canyon.

I decided at that moment that I would fly again. A few months later, in Bisbee, Arizona, I got in the cockpit of a glider, took the controls, and flew.

I had learned a basic truth; nothing is absolutely safe.

Live your life, take all necessary precautions, but follow your heart. Sally Jesse Raphael, on her television program, once asked me if I ever wished I had exercised a little more caution in my life. I told her, "In my office, I've got a poster on my wall that lists the BE-Attitudes. There are things such as Be Loving, Be Warm—but nowhere does it say, 'Be Careful.' I'm not a reckless person. I believe in the value of life. But you can't spend your life in a cave, keeping safe from risk. The greatest risk, in my opinion, is taking no risk at all."

I knew that I wanted to become a solo pilot again someday, but I would need to be certified to use hand controls to run the rudder pedals. From time to time, I flew with friends, sometimes taking the controls. But for now, piloting my motorhome was good enough.

The way I saw it, I had triumphed over more personal adversity than any one person should have to face. If my lifestyle seemed selfish, who could blame me? Hadn't I earned the right to some self-indulgence?

But life is a learning process, and the lessons tend to present themselves whether we seek them or not.

In the summer of 1977, Mayor Tom Glass came into my bar, sat next to me, ordered a beer, and began talking about my responsibility to the community. Crested Butte, he said, had been good to me when I needed help, and I could give something back by filling one of the two vacancies on the town council.

He finally persuaded me, but I was the world's least enthusiastic candidate. My "campaign" speech to the other council members (who were appointing people to fill these positions) focused largely on my doubt that I would do any more than fill out the term, which ran only another four months. They must have liked my looks, however, and I got their unanimous vote.

Thus began my entry into elective politics. Sure, it was no big deal to be on the town council of a little Colorado mountain town, but a major issue was just starting to rise to the surface, and, as fate would have it, entering the council was my first step into the thick of it. Perhaps Tom Glass saw something in me that I was not yet able to recognize in myself.

AMAX, Inc., the largest mining company in the world, was, at that moment, exploring the possibility of building a billion-dollar molybdenum mine on the mountain that forms the backdrop of the town. The mountain's official name was Mount Emmons, but all of the locals called her "The Red Lady" because of the gorgeous crimson hue she takes on at sunset. The mine would be the biggest industrial project in the history of western Colorado.

It is well argued that we, as a nation, need molybdenum. Alloyed with other metals, it makes airplane engines, cars, bicycles, even wheelchairs, lighter and stronger. The project also promised to make townspeople like me, who owned businesses and land, rich from the influx of workers and money.

But as the weeks progressed and more and more AMAX officials came to town, the image that haunted many of us was of the huge molybdenum mine that AMAX operates in Leadville. It is a horrid gash, a scar on the face of Colorado.

That mine erased most of Bartlett mountain, but the worst aspect was the tailings it left behind. Even in a very rich "moly" deposit, only six-tenths of one percent of the rock is moly. The rest is waste rock, including toxic heavy metals such as cadmium. To extract the moly, the raw rock is ground into sand and dumped into a chemical solution that contains arsenic and other nasty chemicals, which leach out the moly and float it to the top. The rest goes into tailings piles, also known by the more descriptive appellation, "slimepits." You can see these old slimepits all over Colorado, quietly leaching toxic gunk into the watersheds of dozens of communities.

Mining and environmental regulation had come a long way since some of those pits were made, and it was unlikely that this mine would be quite as awful as some of its predecessors. But here we were, in one of the most beautiful little towns in Colorado, set in the middle of millions of acres of wilderness, one of the least spoiled, but still easily accessible communities in America. You could literally walk from the town into areas of pristine beauty. It was a town filled with urban dropouts who had come here precisely for this pristine scenery. We had come to see ourselves as stewards of this land, and now were imagining the whole thing being ruined beyond redemption.

So, three weeks after I was elected to the council, I was heading to a council meeting with Ken Hall, the guy everyone acknowledged would be the next mayor, and we started chatting about this potential mine.

"Nobody says no to them," he said glumly. "They have never failed to get permission to put a mine where they want to." He said the best thing the town could hope for was a park or a road to divert the mine-worker traffic around the town, in exchange for being nice and cooperative.

I couldn't believe what I was hearing. After the burns and paralysis, I had put together a successful, happy life, and it was increasingly clear to me that a determined person could do almost anything. I figured that perhaps the reason no one had ever repelled AMAX was that no one had ever tried.

At that moment, I decided to try. To do so, I would have to run for mayor.

For the next three months, I devoted every ounce of energy to running for the job. I studied the sewer system, the garbage system, the traffic—did we need our first traffic light? I parked my wheelchair at the intersection all day, trying to decide. I read planning documents that no one but the planner had read.

I shook every hand in town, several times. It was the most organized, intense campaign in town history. I actually spent upwards of fifty dollars, which surely broke the old record by at least forty-nine dollars.

About three hundred people voted. I won by twenty votes. The battle was on.

The morning after the election, I attended an

"exploratory" meeting held by AMAX officials in Gunnison. The company, as it often does, had hired the biggest names it could: Gordon Allet, former U.S. senator from Colorado, and Wayne Aspinall, Colorado's former U.S. congressman who had chaired the House Interior Committee. They could both be most helpful in greasing the wheels for AMAX before the regulators, but they were just additional insurance. No one had ever stopped a mining company—at least no one we knew about.

The company had two other huge advantages. First, the mine would be located on county land, just outside of the Crested Butte city limits, so we had no apparent jurisdiction. Second, the only federal law that addresses mining rights is the General Mining Act of 1872, which says, essentially, that the best, highest use for public land is mining; that it comes before recreation, forestry, conservation, wildlife, you name it. The gist of the law is that if you want to build a mine on public land, you can. In fact, please do, and you don't even have to bother paying royalties.

For the next four years, we spent vast amounts of time, not to mention about $160,000 of my own money, coming up with ways to overcome these handicaps (my mayor's salary of twenty-five dollars a month didn't quite cover my outlay, but I didn't mind).

Our major tool was the media. It was a classic David-and-Goliath story, and the press ate it up. Typical was a *Time* magazine article titled, "Battle over the Red Lady: A Colorado Shangri-La in a Classic Struggle Against Development," which ran a photo of me, in my wheelchair, in a pristine field of buttercups, pointing to the mine's proposed location.

I was always good for a quote. As I stated in that article, "There are messes all over the West in the name of growth. Big mining companies have no divine right to mine and tear up a community. They'd rape us and leave us bleeding."

I've never believed in subtlety.

I made our case in the *New York Times*, the *San Francisco*

Examiner, the *Washington Post*, on the "Today Show" and "Good Morning America."

You name it, I did it.

The point I made, over and over, is that the public lands are just that: the property of the public. They should be treated as a sacred trust for future generations. While the profits would vanish in weeks in the form of million-dollar bonuses to CEO's and contributions to sympathetic politicians, the slimepits would persist for thousands of years.

I also buttonholed politicos, including Jack Watson, one of President Jimmy Carter's closest aides. Watson was one of the best and brightest in an administration whose greatest strength—and weakness—was that it really gave a damn, in a town where the only measure of achievement is the accumulation of power. (Dick Lamm, Colorado's popular, maverick former governor, describes most politicians as "weathervanes, not compasses.") You generally had no trouble knowing which way the wind was blowing in Washington, but I found the Carter administration a rare exception to that rule.

At any time that I arranged a meeting with Watson, or any of the other staff in the West Wing of the White House, I always went a half-hour early, because it was always interesting to see who showed up.

On one of my early visits, I invited a special friend from Crested Butte, Cathy Sporcich, to join me. I had already learned the layout of the West Wing. We were heading down a hallway toward Vice President Mondale's office, and halfway down, a swarm of people came toward us and suddenly, there was Jimmy Carter. The hallway was so narrow, he literally had to squeeze by me. He stopped, asked me where I was from, we chatted briefly, and then he started to go down the hall again.

"By the way," I piped up, "We really enjoy having your daughter, Amy, come and ski at Crested Butte."

That stopped the whole procession, and we talked a good bit more. I later met Carter on several occasions, and though I never asked him personally to intervene in my dispute with AMAX, I think my acquaintance with him helped my cause; it gave me credibility and helped me to mobilize a lot of people in his administration to work on our behalf.

And we fought on legal fronts. We dug up an obscure, one hundred-year-old state law that gave cities the right to control their watersheds. We set up the Crested Butte Municipal Watershed and began writing restrictive regulations, and even invented a permitting process, because the mine would be smack in the middle of that watershed. If there is one thing that the powers-that-be respect in the West, even above mining, it is water. The town was behind me, too; I won reelection in 1980 capturing ninety percent of the vote.

What Crested Butte lacked in financial strength and jurisdictional authority, it made up for with bright, creative minds, and the intensity of the media spotlight that I helped direct toward our cause. Miles Rademan, our town planner (think of it: a community of less than a thousand people with the audacity to have a planning department!), with both a planning and a law degree, had fought some hairy regulatory battles in other cities and was well versed in the tactics of modern David-vs.-Goliath duels.

Wes Light and Ron Landeck, who had served as Crested Butte's town attorney and special council at various times, were delighted to have the chance to write legal history. They brought in legal scholars and students from all over America, who dug up new legal means to confound AMAX. That was fun, but perhaps more importantly, they were creating legal precedents that would help other little communities fight similar battles against multinational corporations armed with wads of money.

In the meantime, AMAX fought harder and harder to pacify us, promising us concessions and entertaining us royally. But while eating a sumptuous, AMAX-sponsored dinner in "Windows on the World" in New York City, the wonderful words of Mo Udall, chairman of the House Interior Committee, rang in my mind: "If you can't eat their food, drink their liquor, and vote against them, you don't belong in Congress."

We did not send AMAX screaming into the night. This vast organization, with thirteen, full-time congressional lobbyists, was willing to fight us over the long haul, and might well have eventually beat us.

But what we did do was slow them up. In response to our challenges, they were forced to constantly redesign the mine. For example, we made them add a tunnel. Then we made them add a train to haul tailings through it to a valley far away from our watershed. The train, we demanded, would also have to transport the miners to and from work, so they would not disrupt town traffic.

We created many conditions and requests, and in most cases, with other mines, no one had even taken the time to ask. We wanted a lot, because the damage done by a project such as this is virtually irreparable. We wanted them to pay up front, because once the mine has gone bust and the profits have been spent, there would be no one left to pay. Except, of course, the taxpayers, citizens, and wildlife—all of whom are left with the consequences.

By the time they quit, we had barely started.

But quit they did. The recession of 1981 made the bottom drop out of the moly market. The company attributes its withdrawal entirely to that, not to us, but it's clear that our stumbling blocks were the real difference. We slowed AMAX long enough so that the recession could come along and deliver the coup de grâce.

The only legacy AMAX left was the cleaning up of pollution caused by the Keystone Mine, an old lead and zinc mine AMAX had purchased, at a cost of thirteen million dollars. We made them do it. It was a thrill to see Coal Creek clear again for the first time in years. It was about time that a mining company picked up the tab for mine-caused pollution.

To me, it was all a glorious experience, worth a half-dozen Ph.D.'s. The highlight was a big "Bye, Bye AMAX" party we held on the summit of the Red Lady. Almost everyone else hiked up there in their "Bye, Bye AMAX" T-shirts printed especially for the occasion. I hitched a ride up there on a news helicopter that had been dispatched to cover the event. There I sat among my friends, and we laughed, drank, cried, and told the Lady that we loved her.

I was victorious, nationally famous, and transported with happiness.

I had won personal battles before; I had returned, better and stronger, from two terrible accidents through sheer force of will. But this win was even more satisfying, because it was more than just personal. I had stood up for something bigger than myself.

The planet, I remain convinced, has too few defenders, and I often wonder why that is. Is it because no one taught us to care? Is it because saving it, even a piece of it, seems so hopeless against all the forces arrayed against it, all of the incantations and incarnations of that hideous philosophy, "bigger is better?"

That destiny is a matter of choice is not something I learned early in life. For many of us, our destiny is tied to the latest advertising campaign on TV, to the most recent soft drink promotion. The conditioning of prisoners done by the enemies is was called brainwashing. What should we call ads, directed with dizzying rapidity, at children whose babysitters are TV sets?

Has anyone considered what the same media blitz, with the same cunning and genius, directed at responsible parenting, wise use and reuse of our resources, population control, or any of the other ethics and skills the planet needs, could potentially do?

Someday, I hope we find out. The planet can no longer afford to have its most potent and influential information technologies controlled by forces that put the bottom line above all other values. The real issue in the AMAX fight was, as Congresswoman Pat Schroeder of Colorado is fond of saying, "You've got to stand for something, or you are going to fall for everything."

When the next mayoral election rolled around in 1982, it seemed like an afterthought. Sure, I would continue in office, it would be fun to decompress and be a normal, small-town mayor. It never occurred to me that I would lose.

But I did. Townspeople explained to me that it was

clear I would go on to bigger and better things, and there was a sense that I was running around the country being a famous, glamorous person, and didn't realize that the local economy was in a slump due to a snowless winter.

Now I knew what Winston Churchill had felt like. I had done a great job, but that was then, and now is now.

Chapter 14

People who are sensible about love are incapable of it.
—Douglas Yates

I don't give up anything easily. But it sometimes occurred to me, as I was giving AMAX fits, that it was far easier to push around this huge corporation than it was to get Annie to make a commitment to me.

I tried everything. While in the White House, I would have the operator there call her and say, "Hold for a call from the White House." I invited her to swanky parties with the Rockefellers in Denver. She was utterly unimpressed.

She always liked me, and my physical oddities weren't an issue. It was more that I lived and moved in a different world. I am thirteen years older, and was forever jetting off to some pow-wow with a politician, going on TV, closing a business deal.

She was just eighteen when she first met me as a nurse's aide. I would describe her—and she agrees—as innocent and unworldly. For six years, we were friends. Annie would do me favors: get my car outfitted with hand controls, get together casually in Denver. She even came to Crested Butte a couple of times with one of her girlfriends, but our relationship never transcended friendship. Our conversations seemed superficial, and I never really knew what was inside her heart. Sometimes we would go to dinner, and I often tried to get her to go away with me somewhere, but there was always a reason she could not, or would not.

Annie came from a lower–middle class family in Illinois. Her father had walked out when she was five; her mother worked at a dental lab by day and took in ironing at night to make ends meet. It was a rough existence, but it gave Annie a stubborn streak that I admired. She did not want to be smothered by me, and that was one of the reasons I loved her. With my huge ego, I could easily overwhelm a weaker person.

Ironically, what finally won her over was that rarest of events in my life: an admission of defeat. In the fall of 1980, I had called her yet again and asked her to go to dinner.

Again, she demurred and added, "Persistent, aren't you?"

It hurt. I had wanted so much to know her and to get close to her, and it was clear that I was never really important. It felt as if she would only see me if there was nothing better to do. She never wanted to put herself in a position where we had a lot of time together.

I don't recall precisely what I said in response, but it was clear to her from my tone that I'd had enough. I wrote her off—very reluctantly—and determined to get on with my life.

Two weeks later, out of the blue, she called me.

"You haven't called me for a while," she said. "You've talked about taking me to Santa Fe. Is that still a possibility?"

This was only a week before I was scheduled to give some speeches to environmental groups in New Zealand. I had only one free weekend left.

That weekend, everything changed. One of the finest moments of my life was when she got off that airplane in Gunnison, got into my car, and the two of us looked at each other and realized we were in love.

We married nineteen months later, at the foot of the mountain in the "Oh Be Joyful" wilderness area that my lobbying had helped to protect.

I'd like to say that we lived happily ever after, but life, as you may have noticed, is a bit more complex than the average fairy tale.

For starters, I was a bit scared. This was my third marriage, and, as it had before, the image of spending eternity with another person spooked me a little. Though married, we still had the same differences in worldliness and outlook that we'd had before.

But one problem we did not have was the one many people might have suspected: our sexual lives together. Most people might conclude that sex with a burned-up paraplegic is not every young girl's dream. But that was not a factor at all. I am, by nature, a sensual person, a toucher, a holder, a cuddler. While paralysis cancels physical sensation below the waist, the real sex organ—the brain—is above it.

So we became lovers the way any other couple would. One of the advantages of a wheelchair is that you always have somewhere for your loved one to sit. We spent lots of time like that—with her on my lap, watching the waves in Hawaii or the sunset over the Rockies.

Over time, the awkwardness, the fear, went away. As we spent time together, our friendship grew.

Chapter 15

*I have come to the conclusion that politics
are too serious a matter to be left to the politicians.*
—General Charles De Gaulle

Again, life seemed to settle into a comfortable routine, which should, by then, have served as a warning to me that I was about to do something weird.

I served as vice chairman of the National Parks and Conservation Association, testifying before Congress and doing lots of lobbying. I was also nominated and accepted as a member of the American chapter of Club of Rome, the respected environmental organization that drafted the ground-breaking work "Limits to Growth," perhaps the first scholarly treatise to explain in detail why humankind can't keep raping the earth at will. Many other environmental organizations asked me to join and speak on their behalf, and I accepted. I did not know it then, but those early speeches were the preparation for the speaking I'm doing today.

With my Vermont Castings stock and various investments and holdings, I was worth at least three million dollars. I was busy, but I could afford to take breaks now and then, and I did.

One of the groups with which I became involved was the American Wilderness Alliance, now called American Wildlands. Jerry Mallet and Sally Raniey, who founded it, loved river rafting, and invited me to join them on their trips. We ran sections of the Colorado River, but the most memorable was a "V.I.P. tour" that included Bill Moyers of public broadcasting fame and John Oaks, former editorial page editor of the *New York Times*. I joined the trip to float the last part, which included Lava Falls in the

Grand Canyon, one of the biggest and wildest rapids anywhere.

In the campgrounds along the river, during quiet periods when others were off on hikes into side canyons, I read *Explorations of the Colorado River*, by Major John Wesley Powell, who in 1869 became the first white man to float through the Grand Canyon. There are classic photos of this one-armed Civil War veteran standing in a wooden dory as it approached the rapids. In the book, I learned that it was while he was lying in the hospital after his arm had been amputated, that he began dreaming of leaving the civilized world, which brought so much death and destruction, and returning to nature. It was precisely the same feeling I had felt lying in that bed in San Francisco, dreaming of Yosemite, which was, in fact, the first place I visited outside of the city once I was released.

So I felt a great affinity with Powell. And as we approached Lava Falls, and the discussion turned to deciding which of our flotilla of boats would be safest for me, all I could think of was Powell in his wooden dory. In my usual, tactful way, I announced that I'd be taking the dory.

"Uh, I don't know, Mitchell," said one of the boat handlers. This was actually a sort of publicity event—we were trying to bring attention to Glen Canyon Dam's poorly conceived water-release policies, which had badly eroded sensitive beaches to make more electricity for the obscene neon of Las Vegas—and drowning the paraplegic environmentalist wasn't exactly the kind of press these guys wanted. "These inflatables will be a lot more... comfortable."

But a couple of the people had run rivers with me before and knew that I could swim when a boat overturned, so they, and I, prevailed.

Boyd Matson, the NBC newsman, rode in the front of the dory. There was a boatman in the middle and I was in the back. A photo of this crew shows Matson looking scared, the boatman looking worried, and me grinning like an idiot. I figured it was too nice a day to die.

We didn't, but it was a hell of a ride. It was like going into a washing machine and flipping the "spin" cycle on the way in. Ironically, as a "control" freak, nothing thrills me more than losing control to the raging forces of nature.

Then one day, after returning from a two-week solo car trip visiting national parks in the Southwest, I was digging through a ton of accumulated mail and newspapers in my office, and I came across a story stating that Ray Kogovsek, Colorado's Third District congressman, was not going to run for a fourth term.

I looked at it for a long time. The story made it clear that a half-dozen big names were ready to run for the Democratic nomination. Later, West Light came over and joked with me, asking if I were going to run.

"Right," I said. "An environmentalist mayor from an elitist ski town, running in a district full of redneck ranchers and unemployed steelworkers."

He left. I went to bed.

At 3 a.m., I woke up, got a pad and pencil, and wrote down all of the things I would have to do to run for Congress. I decided to do it because of a basic rule I use to govern my life: the only way you can really fail in life is never to try.

I announced.

I organized.

I assembled a team.

Every time a story appeared about the race with no mention of me, I called the reporter to explain that I was, indeed, a serious candidate. Two days later another story would appear, and sure enough, my name would be absent.

In any case, the important thing was to get together with the people who attended the precinct caucuses, held all over the district, usually in someone's home. You needed someone in each of them to speak for you, to get people excited when the time came for them to go from these little meetings to the county assemblies.

I worked the county assemblies like crazy, and no one

took me the least bit seriously. I was not only politically incorrect by the lights of that district, but I looked weird as hell.

When I arrived at the congressional district assembly, the popular wisdom was that I would not even get on the primary ballot. By then, there were three of us in the race. Owen Aspinall, the son of Wayne Aspinall, who had been the district's congressman for twenty-two years, had incredible name recognition: the name Aspinall is legendary in Colorado politics. Then there was Dick Soash, a popular state senator as well as a rancher who wore cowboy boots and was clearly the front runner. And there was me.

By this point, I was at least getting my name in the paper, but it was still clearly Soash and Aspinall's race. You needed twenty percent of the votes of the five hundred delegates to get on the primary ballot. If you didn't, you were history.

I remember talking with the most astute political analyst on the scene, Cindy Parmenter, political reporter for the *Denver Post*. "You're a nice guy, Mitchell, and you've worked hard," she said, "but I don't think you're going to get on the ballot."

Dick Soash had already told his supporters that if he did not come in first in the balloting, he would not run. When the votes were all counted, Soash got forty-three percent, I got forty-two, Aspinall got fifteen percent. Soash was mad as hell, and we were off to the races.

I came so close to Soash because no one had been taking me seriously. Now they were. With the unions and ranchers on his side, hardly anyone believed I stood a chance.

But I worked as hard as I have ever worked: sixteen hours a day, seven days a week, campaigning. I took a total of nine days off in eleven months. I set up a campaign office in Crested Butte, but I spent most of the time in an airplane I had purchased. Because Colorado's Third Congressional District is one of the largest in the United states, the airplane turned out to be indispensable.

At the beginning, people had no idea what to make of me. I remember one guy, a rancher in a cowboy hat and boots, pointedly asking me, how was I going to get to vote on time in my wheelchair?

I told him that I had been to Washington more than one hundred times to lobby for various causes and was very familiar with the layout of Capitol Hill.

"Between the Canon House Office Building—which is where they put most of the freshmen congressmen—and the Capitol, there's a tunnel," I told him. "And that tunnel runs downhill to the Capitol. With this wheelchair, the only member of congress who'll beat me to the floor will be one on a skateboard."

The crowd loved it. So did I.

It had been suggested that I use as my official campaign motto: "He's not just another pretty face." It summed up what I was trying to show: that my handicaps could be an asset, not a liability. But we went with something a little more traditional: "There's nothing he can't do."

In retrospect, it might have been wise to go with the more outrageous slogan.

I won the primary and confounded every political pundit in the state. It was a squeaker—I won by three thousand votes—but I won. Soash never congratulated me, never even spoke to me after the victory, and all the promises we had made to each other about party unity evaporated.

In the general election two months later, I was defeated by Mike Strang, who, next to me, was my favorite candidate in the whole race. Like me, he was an odd, interesting duck: He had been homeschooled by his parents and went from their ranch directly to Princeton, where be became an outstanding scholar. Politically, he took a fairly conservative line, but was actually one of the more enlightened state legislators during his term in the statehouse, and Annie and I genuinely liked him and his wife, Kit.

In retrospect, there were two main reasons I lost: I had made a noble but probably stupid pledge to take no political action committee money, and the Reagan coattail effect was brutal to all Democrats in 1984. Comparatively, I did rather well: while the President got seventy percent of the statewide vote, Strang got just fifty-seven percent. Aside from the coattail effect, Strang was also aided by a huge infusion of money from the National Rifle Association and other conservative groups.

But I tell people today that I didn't lose that race in 1984. I tell them that, yes, my opponent got a few more votes than I did and that hurt, but the wonderful lesson I learned is that the only losers are the ones who don't get in the race. I love to quote Theodore Roosevelt, who said that the only real losers in life are the people who end their lives, "having tasted neither victory nor defeat."

Running for Congress was worth at least three Ph.D.'s. I honestly believe that there is no such thing as defeat; that there is victory in trying, in learning, in doing what you can. I was able to convince ninety-three thousand people that a burned-up, fingerless guy in a wheelchair would represent them better than an able-bodied chap with a nice complexion.

To me, that's a victory.

My sweetest memory is the political endorsement I got from William Grider, the political editor of *Rolling Stone* magazine, who said that I was "indisputably the ugliest politician in America."

As he put it, "...this guy is a little weird and wonderfully original, and I hope he gets elected to Congress. That assembly seems permanently overpopulated by fools and knaves, hacks and drones, the TV hot-dogs who hide behind blow-dry hairdos and vacant smiles. The Capitol would be staggered by the mere presence of this man's indomitable spirit."

Chapter 16

It is courage the world needs, not infallibility...
Courage is always the surest wisdom.
                                    —Sir Wilfred Grenfell

I had put a thousand chores on hold while running for office. Now it was time to catch up.

First came paying back the $450,000 loan I had used to finance my campaign. As any politician knows, it is much easier to pay off a campaign debt if you win. Since I had not, I ended up selling all of my remaining Vermont Castings stock and covered virtually the whole amount myself. I had once owned a third of the company, now I was completely out.

Second, I nearly died. This was not a chore, but came as the result of performing one, and was yet another example—as if I needed one—of the fact that taking control can save your life.

The chore was getting my eyelids fixed so they would close more completely. Burned skin tends to shrink over time, and my eyelids had become too short to close completely, so Mark Gorney was going to correct that at St. Francis Hospital in San Francisco. As part of his thirty-year project to make me look like Mel Gibson, he also planned to do some cosmetic work on my somewhat caved-in nose. The extra skin and cartilage needed for both procedures would be taken from my ears.

My eyelids would be sewn shut for a week. Some people might think this is a horrible fate, but I was looking forward to it. Again, we tend to experience what we expect to experience. If you think you'll hate something, guess what? You almost always will.

During the preoperative procedures, I asked for a liberal

dose of morphine. I had learned, after twenty-five or so operations, that I was gradually building up a tolerance.

The anesthesiologist complied. But just as he was about to administer the general anesthetic, I felt my heart start to speed up. It was no longer beating, it was humming like a runaway engine.

Again, people often go limp in hospitals. I can imagine that some people, rationalizing that "I'm not a doctor, I am sure they know what they are doing" would have let their heart continue to fibrillate wildly as the general anesthetic kicked in and they became too groggy to mention it even if they wanted to.

But this, I hope you've learned by now, is not my style.

"Hold it," I said to Mark. "I think there is something wrong with my heart."

Mark has learned through the years to listen to me, so they slapped a blood-pressure cuff on me. My pressure had gone through the roof! Quickly, they gave me an "anti-morphine," which cancels, instantly, the morphine in the bloodstream.

My heart calmed down.

In any case, the operation got pushed back four hours.

The next day, Arthur Jackson, a friend from Aspen who had helped in my congressional campaign, called from Arizona. He had been attending a personal development seminar led by a guy named Tony Robbins. The big moment of these seminars was something called the firewalk, where you stroll barefoot over hot coals.

In my usual nonjudgmental style, I told Arthur that Robbins was crazy, and he, Arthur, was crazy if he walked in this firepit, and they were both crazy if they thought I would ever do such a thing. I had had my fire experience, thank you.

But he insisted that Robbins really wanted me to come down. I said, it sounds weird, but I'll think about it. He said no, Robbins wants you to come right now.

"Look," I said. "My eyes are sewn shut. I can't go anywhere."

"He really wants to see you," Arthur insisted. "He wants you to speak at his seminar. Have someone put you on an airplane. You don't need to be able to see." He pushed and pushed, and finally, after three days of calls—the more I told him what a mess I was, the more they wanted me—he hit the right buttons: I would definitely meet some unusual people, and this might be a good place to raise some money to pay off my campaign debt.

Friday morning, four days after the operation, they yanked a couple of stitches out of one eye so that I could barely peek through it. Annie drove me and our dog, Hannibal, to Los Angeles, where we spent the first night; then we headed to Carefree, Arizona, which is near Phoenix.

The biggest convention in Phoenix history—I don't know for what—was happening that night, and a hotel room could not be found, so Annie and I spent the night in the car. So you can't imagine a more ragged-looking creature than me the next day, when I was introduced to Tony Robbins. Burned, in a wheelchair, eyes sewn shut, sutures in my ears, rumpled, and dead tired from two long days in the car, I am sure I looked like the perfect guy to help him whip up three hundred inspiration-hungry people.

But he and everyone around him were fascinated by me. I had a reputation as a survivor, a guy who could do the impossible, and that's what these seminars were all about.

So the next day I spoke to the folks at his seminar. They invited me to stay, and a surgeon, who was taking part in the seminar, cleaned and looked after my fresh surgical scars.

Three days after I arrived, firewalk night rolled around. Three beds of mesquite coals were prepared, ranging from twelve to forty feet long. This was the hottest fire Tony had ever used. I was about eight feet away, and it was so intense that I was worried it would somehow mess up the plastic surgery work that had just been done on me, so I had them back me up.

I planned only to watch, for a couple of reasons. First, I don't walk. Second, I had had my fire experience. Third, I didn't need this routine anyway. The whole idea behind this is that if you can walk on fire, you prove to yourself that you can do damn near anything, that any limitations in your life are probably self-imposed. I had already figured that out in my own way, so who needed this?

People started walking through the coals. As they emerged, they were exultant. No one was burned. I'd guess 250 people did it.

I don't even remember how it came about, but suddenly, there I was at the end of this bed of coals in my wheelchair, taking off my shoes and socks and saying to Tony and another friend, Tom Crum, "One of you grab me under the right arm, one under the left, lift me up and turn me around, because we are going to do this backward."

And that's what we did.

I had more contact with the coals than anyone else. While the other workshop participants had stepped through the coals, I was literally dragged through them. When we got to the other side, I could see the two dark trails where my heels had gone.

I did not have a single burn.

What did it mean?

A lot of scientists are skeptical that anything mystical is involved. There are elaborate theories about perspiration on the feet repelling the heat, through a principle similar to touching a wet finger to a hot iron and not being burned. These theories might be true—although I was in contact for quite a while.

But even if it is not literal magic, it certainly is a potent metaphor. It is a visible illustration of the power anyone has to face when confronted by a frightening barrier and discover that there was no real reason to fear it at all.

I firmly believe that most barriers are self-imposed. We first get them from society—you can't do that, that's immoral, that's crazy, no one in our family does that, and so on—but we forget that we have the power to accept or reject these barriers. We treat them as if they are immovable, immutable, when, in fact, they may be silly, cause unnecessary misery, or just be plain nonexistent.

To illustrate this with one more vivid example: back in the 1950s, it was widely accepted that no one would ever run a four-minute mile—that was, simply, something that human beings were not capable of pulling off. Then, in 1954, Roger Bannister ran one in three minutes, fifty-nine and four-tenths' seconds. The *next* year, some fifty people broke the four-minute "barrier." Now, high school athletes break it routinely. Bannister demonstrated that the barrier was not real, but the remarkable thing is that any of those fifty people could have figured it out on their own. They didn't *need* to wait for Bannister to show them the fallacy of it.

An even more poignant and modern example is the story of Cliff Young, a rather unsuccessful sixty-five-year-old farmer from Australia, who showed up at the starting line of the annual five hundred kilometer Sydney-to-Melbourne race. Hundreds of people show up at the start of that race every year, but this was the first time anyone had arrived in his farm boots and bib overalls, causing the more polite of the bystanders to smile and the ruder ones to ridicule the old guy.

They were still hooting as the gun sounded, and the runners zoomed ahead of Cliff. He did not even run correctly. He just shuffled along in his gum boots. And at night, when the six-hour break came, which everyone knew you had to take to have the stamina to win, Cliff was too stupid even to understand that. When he finally arrived at the break point, he just kept running. And that was the last any of the other runners ever saw of him. Cliff Young broke the Sydney-to-Melbourne record by some twelve hours, and no one was laughing anymore.

By the next year, everyone was shuffling like Cliff Young. It became the preferred style of ultra-long distance running. Quite a few people broke Cliff's record, thanks to what they learned from him.

I had already discovered this: that it's the folks who

don't pay attention to what "everybody knows" who often succeed in life.

But it was wonderful to see the faces of the 250 people who walked through the firepit that night. I suspected that, from that point on, it would be difficult to convince any of them that he or she faced an insurmountable obstacle.

This is not to say that every obstacle can simply be "walked across" like that firepit. Often, tremendous energy and hard work are required, and the obstacle may need to be surmounted in a way no one could have guessed.

I remember a kid back in Crested Butte. His name was David, he was the son of the owner of Sancho's, the town's Mexican restaurant, and he was about seven years old. With that distinctive honesty of kids—which can be endearing or obnoxious, depending upon how one takes it—he was pointing out that I was "a mess."

"You don't even have any hands. You probably can't do anything," he told me.

"I have been told that before," I responded. "But I can fly an airplane, drive a car, dress myself. That seems like good stuff to me."

"Okay," he said. "Pick up this." He pointed to a quarter on the table. I hadn't picked up my change. What the hell? You need to leave a tip anyway, and besides, it was too much trouble.

You've got to hand it to this kid. He had picked a tough assignment. Fingers are very handy for dealing with coins. And when it came to paying for something, my normal habit is to hold out a collection to a clerk and have him pick the right ones from my hand. But there it was on the table. The gauntlet had been thrown down.

I studied the situation. Grasping it with one hand was clearly impossible. But it seemed to me that if I pressed on the edge very hard with my right thumb, I could make the coin stand on its edge. I did this, pinched the coin between both hands, and handed it to him.

I was pretty proud of myself. The challenge had been to pick up the coin, and I had done it.

But David was having none of it. "You cheated!" he said. "You were supposed to use only one hand!"

"I don't recall that being part of the challenge you laid out to me," I replied. "You dared me to pick up the coin, and I did."

He still wasn't impressed. He wasn't satisfied, because I wasn't doing it in the only way that he had learned it should be done. I was not playing by the established rules. I was not solving the problem the way everyone else had solved it.

So:

Many barriers—like the firepit—that we are told are real, don't exist at all.

Of the ones that do have some substance—like the sub-four-minute mile, which is no mean feat to accomplish—many can be vanquished through sheer effort.

And of the ones that seem even more formidable—like picking up a quarter with no fingers, or having a wonderful, accomplished life though you are burned and in a wheelchair—most can be surmounted through effort *plus* a willingness to dig under them, go around them, hop over them, or otherwise use one's ingenuity to defeat them.

It's not what happens to you. It's what you do about it.

Chapter 17

Good people are good because they've come to wisdom through failure.
—William Saroyan.

When Tony asked me to talk at his workshops, I had no "speech" except for a real rabble-rouser about farm prices and unemployment remedies in Colorado's Third District.

But I have always been pretty good at speaking off the cuff. I simply told Tony's groups my story—the funny parts, the tough parts, the triumphant parts. People loved it. Most people have scars, too. Just because they are not as visible as mine—maybe they were scarred by abusive parents, or dyslexia, or some other invisible malady—doesn't mean they are not real, or that they can't learn from someone who has overcome his own, more visible scars.

Tony invited me back to each of his annual meetings. Looking back, that was the real start of my speaking career. The hundreds and hundreds of political speeches, talks I had given on disability issues, my testimonies before Congress and other committees, and countless interviews, all came together. The cumulative experience worked. Doing things again and again breeds a familiarity, a competence. So often, we ignore life's little homilies. It is sad, because practice often does make perfect.

In June of 1985, I moved to Denver and began doing TV commentary. While a guy with a face like a bad road might seem a poor candidate for such a job, the fact is, Susan Landess, an Emmy-award-winning TV producer and publicist and great buddy during my time in Colorado, told me I was "mediagenic." With my odd looks and wheelchair and a whole bunch of experience at getting past the superficial, I stand out against the sea of same-face, same-sound people we so often see on the box.

And, naturally, I am a captivating speaker.

More and more, I was being asked to speak to various groups. Many times I was offered fees, which I turned down. I spoke before environmental groups, handicap advocacy groups, and several congressional committees considering environmental legislation.

What flipped the switch for me was a woman approaching me in a supermarket. She was putting together a convention for temporary employment agencies and knew of me and wondered if I would speak. I was lukewarm, until she mentioned it paid two hundred dollars. Imagine, I thought. A two-hundred-dollar check and a free meal to boot!

By the fall of 1987, I realized that I had a wonderful opportunity. I saw that I could make my living by doing something that I had always, gladly, done for free—sharing the lessons I had learned about life, telling people that it's not what happens to you, it's what you do about it.

I committed myself to becoming a professional public speaker. I knew that it would be a challenge. If I were Ronald Reagan, Oliver North, John Elway, I could ride along on name recognition. W Mitchell would be harder sell.

And again, people were happy to confirm my doubts. "It's really impossible, Mitchell. There are too many obstacles. Who is going to hire you to speak—not just for fifty bucks, but at a rate that can support you—when all of these other famous people with compelling messages are out there competing against you?"

I was starting to believe this. I felt stuck. How does a person start this kind of thing?

But I wasn't stuck long. I had two things going for me:

One, I had committed myself to becoming a public speaker. Commitment is the first, most vital component of anything we wish to accomplish. David Brower, my friend, guide, and hero (I don't have many heroes. I respect many people, but I have few real heroes), is the father of the modern environmental movement. He was the first full-time staffer for the Sierra Club, when its membership was primarily hikers and birdwatchers. He later created Friends of the Earth, and today chairs the Earth Island Institute. He has inspired millions to put their arms around Mother Earth and show her they love her. One of the messages and quotes I have heard him use again and again, and that is carried deep within me always, is from W. N. Murray (you've got to love a guy with a first name like that), the Scottish explorer and mountaineer, who put it forth in a compelling statement:

"Concerning all acts of initiative and creation, there is one elementary truth, the ignorance of which kills countless ideas and splendid plans: that the moment one definitely commits oneself, Providence moves, too. All sorts of things occur to help one, that would otherwise never have occurred. A whole stream issues from the decision, raising in one's favor all manner of unforeseen incidents and meetings and material assistance which no man could have dreamed would have come his way. I have learned a deep respect for one of Goethe's couplets: 'Whatever you can do, or dream you can, begin it. Boldness has genius, power, and magic in it.'"

The second was that, coupled with my commitment, I understood how important it was to act, to *do something* even if I was not sure it was the right thing. Walter Anderson, the editor of *Parade Magazine* and a good friend of mine, has written a book called *The Greatest Risk of All*, in which he says the greatest risk is to take action. Looking back on my life, I saw that this had been the key to my success. Even when I was not sure what I should do, I acted. I did something. If that didn't work, I did something else.

Soon I went to a meeting of the National Speakers Association, which gave me information about the profession of speaking—preparing a brochure, setting fees, getting dates.

Slowly the dates began coming. As I spoke more and more, my speech evolved. It is still evolving; but here is what I always include:

I talk about the two big bumps in my life. I talk about how difficult they were. I talk about how dearly I wanted to quit and how richly I deserved to.

I talk about change: how it can eat you up or help you grow.

And I tell a variety of stories about remarkable people.

One of them is about Ken Campbell, an athlete who smashed his car into a fuel truck and was burned even more extensively than I was. Doctors said he would die; he didn't. They said he would never walk again; he did. They said he would never run again; he did. They said, above all, he could not possibly achieve his lifelong dream: of completing the Ironman Triathalon in Hawaii. With an approximately two-mile swim, a 113-mile bicycle ride, and a twenty-six-mile running race, it is the most grueling endurance contest on the planet.

He did.

He came in dead last.

That description of his finish is apropos, as the effort very nearly killed him.

I talk about how I watched him cross that line with tears streaming down my face. He wasn't in the same race as the other athletes. He was in a different kind of race, one I knew very well.

And he had won.

Another way of looking at it is described by Ken Blanchard, of *One-Minute Manager* fame. He talks about people who go through life as if they are playing a tennis game by watching only the scoreboard and never the court. He often asks the question: "When you take your last breath, are you going to be sorry you haven't made more money?"

While my speaking career began to take off, I did something I had wanted to do for years: I got a master's degree in public administration at the University of Colorado. I did the program in a year, taking on a heavy classload. Today, that diploma hangs proudly in my office, right next to my high school equivalency diploma.

But while both Annie and I were excelling in our

newfound interests—she in anthropology studies at the University of Colorado, and me in my speaking—we seemed to drift further apart, sometimes not seeing each other for days. She was studying furiously. One of her qualities is that she wants all she can get from a class, and she was a straight "A" student.

We spent less and less time working on our relationship. It was not so much that we had tension or difficulty, for we virtually never fought or argued. It was more that a distance had grown up between us.

The physical part of the relationship, in particular, I let slide, and it is my regret to this day that I did not consciously invest myself more in that.

In the spring of 1990, we talked about that distance, but I did little to address it. By fall, it was only her willingness to give it another try that allowed us to continue. In the spring, we made a real effort and had a wonderful trip to Australia together, but I was still focusing harder on what was missing than on what we still had. We divorced in the winter of 1992.

It seems odd that I, who so many others see as one who has mastered everything, allowed a marriage that had an abundance of good qualities and no terrible faults, to slip away, but I did. Today, Annie and I are good friends and are groping for a new way to relate to each other after our divorce.

If I could write the prescription for a good relationship, it would be for people to work hard to understand each other, to agree to be creative, to remember all the things that brought them together, and the things they have learned in their time together, and not just allow the relationship to coast. It's like a car: if you don't steer it, you can wind up in places you don't want to be.

I began this book by pointing out that I am not a saint, not perfect. I have figured out a lot of things, and I have helped many people. But we all have areas that we can work on; letting Annie slip away showed me some of my areas in bold relief. I still have many things to learn.

Chapter 18

Man is what he believes.
—Anton Chekhov

The human brain is like a computer.

At birth, the memory banks are nearly blank. We have innate programming that allows us to breathe and suckle, but 99.9999 percent of the vast storage capability of our mental computers is untouched, waiting to be filled.

And man, is it ever filled.

For the rest of your life, the world around you will shovel data into those hungry storage banks.

Some of the data is good. "Don't run out into a busy street." "Eat your vegetables, they're good for you."

But a great deal of it, in most cases, is not so good.

"Big boys don't cry." "You can't fight city hall." "Can't you do anything right?"

Much of this negative data is not so baldly stated, but is observed and stored nonetheless. If the people in your family never show anger, the message you store is, "Showing anger is awful and must be avoided at all costs." If your parents get divorced, the message is, "Parents get divorced," and, in fact, numerous studies have shown that children of divorced parents are far more likely to get divorced themselves. If your older brothers become criminals and wind up in jail, the message is, "Children in this family break laws and go to jail."

Most of the information is loaded before you have developed any ability to discriminate. And once it settles into the bottom strata, the core memory of your mental computer, it becomes increasingly difficult to erase it and replace it with good stuff.

That's why my favorite speaking venue is not an AT&T

meeting or an association's convention that happily shells out my standard fee, which is more than most people earn in a month. Rather, it's the barn at the Griffith Center, outside of Denver, where I speak for free. It is a center for kids who have literally been thrown on the junkpile: they have been beaten, abused, neglected, thrown out, and this center is their last chance.

Many of these kids have been "programmed," in a million ways, both direct and subtle, to believe that life has stacked the deck against them and that only a chump wastes time trying to learn how to make a contribution.

And then they see me.

A mutilated face. No fingers. A wheelchair. And I am a happy man, a man who had every excuse to be miserable and refused them all.

Every time I stand in front of kids, I am transported back in time to that day years ago when I walked by the playground, heard the chant of "Monster, monster," and longed to speak to those kids and gently show them how wrong they were. I take a moment and catch my breath, because my dream is coming true. I'm here. I'm talking to them. I've got their attention.

I tell them about my accidents. I explain, in great detail, the many opportunities I had to quit and just how and why I refused to take them.

But I don't just talk about myself.

I tell them about Roger Crawford, a remarkable speaker and a good friend of mine. Roger was born with birth defects including a missing foot and hands shaped like lobster claws. I tell them how he refused to quit too. Roger has won NCAA tennis championships (I'm not talking about "handicapped" championships; he has beaten some of the best amateur players in the world), and today teaches tennis professionally as well as sharing his message with the rest of the world as a speaker.

Roger's mother told him something when he was young, something that set the tone for his life. She told him, yes, the package arrived a bit disheveled; the paper was torn, the tape had come unstuck in a few places. But there was a gift inside, and the gift was in good shape.

And I tell them about John Thompson, the eighteen-year-old North Dakota farmboy who was on the farm by himself while his parents visited a friend in the hospital. He was doing his chores, which included loading grain into the barn.

He remembers turning on the auger, a huge screw inside a cylinder that carries grain into a silo. His shirttail was hanging out. It got caught in the auger and began pulling him into the machinery.

He resisted. He fought. But it pulled him harder, and harder. He does not remember much else, but he was spun five times, and then thrown to the ground.

He looked to his right, and saw that his right arm was gone, but he didn't quit. He struggled to his feet, standing there, shaking. He looked to his left. His left arm was gone, too. He did not quit.

He ran 400 yards up the hill to his house. With what little was left of one of his arms, he tried, and tried again, to open the sliding glass door. When he couldn't, once again, he refused to quit. He ran around to the side door and managed to open the screen door; he still does not remember how.

Once inside the kitchen, he knocked the phone off the cradle and tried punching the buttons with his nose, but when that didn't work, he didn't quit. He looked around, found a pencil, and picked it up in his teeth, and pressed buttons on the phone with the eraser. He called his cousin's house, and when the cousin answered, he shouted, "This is John! Get help, quickly, I've had a terrible accident!" Then, he had the presence of mind to pick up the receiver with his teeth and hang up, remembering that on their party line, if he didn't break the connection, his cousin could not make a call.

Then, John Thompson, this eighteen-year-old high school senior, this average kid who got C's in his classes and had never impressed anyone as anything special, went into the bathroom and sat in the bathtub so that he wouldn't bleed on his mother's rug. When the paramedics pulled back the shower curtain, they were so shaken that he had to calm them down, telling them where his arms were and where there was ice in the refrigerator, and garbage sacks in which to pack them.

His arms were reattached in a six-hour operation. When, weeks later, a reporter asked him how it felt to be a hero, the question seemed to baffle him.

"I'm no hero," he said sincerely. "I did what anyone would have done."

He had a point. He was, and is a regular kid, who has the same resources any of us have.

And I'm a regular guy, who has the same resources you do. The point I make to these kids is that we are not heroes, we are not different from you. We just chose to do what we needed to do. You can, too.

I can't help everyone. But some of these kids—these beautiful kids, with strong bodies and active minds—have just enough sensitivity left to see the significance of what I am and of what I am saying to them. Sometimes, and they are magical times, I know that I have gotten to them in time. The core memory is not entirely buried under reams of negativity. There is a chance for my message to get through.

The biggest fee I have ever been paid as a speaker was at the first talk I ever gave at the center. I did not know much about the place, and agreed to speak without a real clue.

As I drove there, I worried. Here I was, starting my speaking career, unsure of myself, unsure if this speech that I had crafted for adults would mean anything to kids, particularly hardened kids like these.

I finished my talk, and by then could plainly see that I had made an impact; I could see it on those faces looking back at me.

But the final confirmation—the greatest fee—was the reaction of a thirteen-year-old kid, clearly from the inner city, who came to me after the speech with tears in his eyes.

He told me that he had tried to commit suicide three times.

I was amazed at his story, but from the way he told it, it was clearly true. But then he said that if he ever felt like doing something like that again, he was just going to stop and remember what I had said that day.

Now both of us had tears in our eyes.

Epilogue

W

Well, Mitchell, it was quite a story and I enjoyed it. I am inspired—I am moved. And I'm glad you and Brad made your story available.

But I'm not sure that I can do the things you've written about. Maybe you have a special set of genes, or you've learned things that I could never understand.

Well, my friends, I am here to tell you that I am no different from you. I could be a little smarter. Probably not as smart. Not much different, though.

The key for all of us who want to change, who want to make a difference, is *to act*. To do something. Anything. That's the key that will unlock the door to a future unimagined by so many people.

If you can't think of what action to take, how about one of these:

Join a group that's already doing something. Don't just join—participate. Think about what you care about—the environment, people who haven't had the opportunities you've had—there is a lot to do.

Become a Big Sister or a Big Brother. With more and more single-parent families, there are lots of kids who could use a friend. You may be surprised to see who benefits more.

There are countless programs that take meals to older people, teach others how to read, support family planning, give those without homes some support in one of the most desperate and degrading moments of their lives.

Sometimes we're stuck in life because of a major disappointment or loss. We feel powerless, unable to do anything. Just one act, anything you can think of, can restart your engine—recharge your battery.

Just because you're out of work doesn't mean you can't

begin a physical-fitness program. Just because you're out of love doesn't mean you can't improve your job skills. By getting better in one area, you'll help your self-esteem, which may unlock the door to new relationships, and perhaps point yourself in a new direction. Is it easy? Perhaps not. But as someone has said, "Easy doesn't do it."

DO SOMETHING NOW.
If not you, who?
If not here, where?
If not now, when?

—Theodore Roosevelt

—*W Mitchell*